ILLUSTRATED
TODAY'S JAPAN
[自然・社会編]

ILLUSTRATED
TODAY'S JAPAN

1st edition 1988
9th edition 2000

Printed in Japan

About this Book

1) Layout

   This book consists of the following five sections
(1) The Nation of Japan; (2) The Lifestyle of the Japanese; (3) Transportation and Communications; (4)
Industry; (5) Politics and Economics, and many short
articles introducing particular aspects of the country's
traditional arts and crafts, performing arts, festivals,
and food, this book is an information-packed essence
of things Japanese.

2)Japanese Words

   All the Japanese words in this book have been
romanized in accordance with the revised Hepburn
system. Except for the names of places and people, all
Japanese words are printed in italics except where
they appear in headings or bold type. Long vowels are
indicated by a line above, as in *'shintō';* and, since e's
are pronounced "ay" in Japanese, e's at the ends of
words are marked with an acute accent, as in *'saké'*
(pronounced "sahkay").

Dear Readers:

This book provides a concise summary of Japan's geography, lifestyle, transportation and communications, industry, politics and economy, and has been edited to provide a broad-based and fundamental understanding of the major aspects of current-day Japan. For those who wish to learn more about a specific area, a reference page is offered for the previously published volumes of the "A Look into Japan" illustrated book series, designed to be utilized as an index for the entire series.

"Today's Japan" is designed to present in this single volume a wide range of useful information to tourists, businessmen and other people who need or want to find out more about Japan. We hope this book will serve the cause of addressing the growing global interest in Japan and the Japanese people.

✳ CONTENTS ✳

THE NATION OF JAPAN
日本の国土
●

THE LIFESTYLE OF THE JAPANESE
日本人の生活
●

TRANSPORTATION AND COMMUNICATIONS
交通と通信
●

INDUSTRY
産業
●

POLITICS
AND
ECONOMICS
政治・経済
●

THE NATION
OF
JAPAN

·

日本の国土

OVERVIEW

Japan is an island nation lying to the east of the Asian continent. It is comprised of some 3,600 islands, clustered around the four major isles of *Hokkaidō, Honshū, Shikoku* and *Kyūshū*, including many which are small and uninhabited. Total land area is 377,000 km^2, or about 1/25th the size of the United States. The population of Japan is about 120 million people.

The Japanese island chain stretches in a bow-shaped configuration along the edge of the Asian continent, from the northeast to the southwest. It covers a span from 20 to 45 degrees north latitude to 123 to 154 degrees east longitude. In terms of distance, this is about 3,300 km from the northern tip at Cape *Sōya,* to the western extremity at *Yonaguni* Island. As a result, Japan is distinguished by a highly diversified climate, ranging from the bitter cold of the northern regions, to the sub-tropical heat of the southern islands.

About 75% of the Japanese land mass is mountainous or hilly terrain, while 67% of the country's surface is covered with forests. Japan has about 200 volcanoes, with historical records indicating past eruptions for about 60 of them. The nation's highly complex and fascinating topography is due in great part to such volcanic activity.

The majority of the nation lies in temperate zones, resulting in clear seasonal changes. It is literally surrounded by water, with the Pacific Ocean lying to the East, the Japan Sea to the West, the Sea of Okhotsk to the North, and the East China Sea to the south. As a result, while Japan belongs to the cultural zone of Southeast Asia, it is also somewhat isolated, and has been able to cultivate its own distinct civilization. The unique nature of the country is closely linked to these geographical conditions.

The Map of Japan

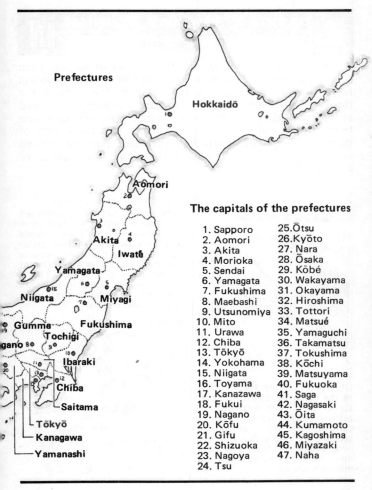

Prefectures

Hokkaidō

Aomori

Akita

Iwate

Yamagata

Niigata

Miyagi

Gumme

Fukushima

Tochigi

gano

Ibaraki

Chiba

Saitama

Tōkyō

Kanagawa

Yamanashi

The capitals of the prefectures

1. Sapporo	25. Ōtsu
2. Aomori	26. Kyōto
3. Akita	27. Nara
4. Morioka	28. Ōsaka
5. Sendai	29. Kōbé
6. Yamagata	30. Wakayama
7. Fukushima	31. Okayama
8. Maebashi	32. Hiroshima
9. Utsunomiya	33. Tottori
10. Mito	34. Matsué
11. Urawa	35. Yamaguchi
12. Chiba	36. Takamatsu
13. Tōkyō	37. Tokushima
14. Yokohama	38. Kōchi
15. Niigata	39. Matsuyama
16. Toyama	40. Fukuoka
17. Kanazawa	41. Saga
18. Fukui	42. Nagasaki
19. Nagano	43. Ōita
20. Kōfu	44. Kumamoto
21. Gifu	45. Kagoshima
22. Shizuoka	46. Miyazaki
23. Nagoya	47. Naha
24. Tsu	

When the islands are viewed from the bottom of the sea, it can be clearly seen that the peaks of a huge submarine mountain range from the land mass which is Japan. According to the theory of plate-tectonics, the Japanese archipelago is located at the point where the Pacific submarine plate and Asian continental plate collide. This theory claims that the activity of these plates separated Japan from the Asian continent millions of years ago, gradually forming the Japanese island chain as we know it today.

The Plate-Tectonics Theory

The earth's surface is comprised of several huge rock formation sections known as "plates." While the core sections of these plates are stable, the crusts are unstable at the sections where different plates come into contact. This is said to be the cause of earthquakes, volcanic eruptions, and other natural phenomena.

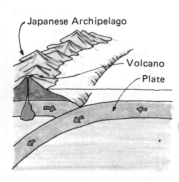

Japanese Archipelago

Volcano

Plate

Nauman Elephant

Bighorn sheep

Discoveries of the fossil remains of the Nauman Elephant (ancestor of the Indian elephant), the bighorn sheep (ancestor of the caribou) and other animal life support the theory that the Japanese islands and the Asian continent were connected some two million years ago.

Japan One Billion Years Ago
Totally incorporated in the Asian continent.

Japan 100 Million Years Ago
A lake formed in the present location of the Japan Sea.

Japan 50 Million Years Ago
The lake gradually expanded in size.

Japan One Million Years Ago
The configuration of the current Japanese island chain was more or less complete.

The Japan Trough — It is from here that the Pacific plate initiates its thrust beneath the Asian plate.

Japan Today
Pulled off in all directions by the collision of the Asia and Pacific plates.

日本の地形   山脈と火山帯

The majority of Japan's hilly country and mountain ranges run down the middle of the island chain, much like a human backbone, while the country's 200 or so volcanoes can be neatly divided into seven volcanic zones. The distribution of these mountain ranges and volcanic zones is thought to have a close relationship with the formation of the Japanese land mass.

Major Japanese Mountain Ranges and Volcanic Zones

A. Chishima Volcanic Zone
B. Nasu Volcanic Zone
C. Chōkai Volcanic Zone
D. Fuji Volcanic Zone
E. Norikura Volcanic Zone
F. Hakusan Volcanic Zone
G. Kirishima Volcanic Zone

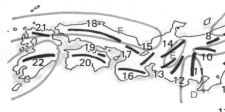

10. Mikuni Mountain Range
11. Kantō Mountains
12. Akaishi Mountain Range (Southern Alps)
13. Kiso Mountain Range (Central Alps)
14. Hida Mountain Range (Northern Alps)
15. Suzuka Mountain Range
16. Kii Mountains
17. Tamba Mountains
18. Chūgoku Mountains
19. Sanuki Mountain Range
20. Shikoku Mountains
21. Tsukushi Mountains
22. Kyūshū Mountains

1. Kitami Mountains
2. Hidaka Mountain Range
3. Teshio Mountains
4. Yūbari Mountains
5. Kitakami Mountains
6. Ōu Mountain Range
7. Dewa Mountains
8. Echigo Mountain Range
9. Abukuma Mountains

Major Japanese Mountains by Region and Altitude (meters)

B. Central Honshū

D. Hokkaidō

A. Southwest Honshū
(including Kyūshū)

C. Northeast Honshū

1.	Mt. Miyanouradaké	1,935	12.	Mt. Asama	2,568
2.	Mt. Kirishima	1,700	13.	Mt. Mihara	764
3.	Mt. Aso	1,592	14.	Mt. Tanigawa	1,978
4.	Mt. Ishizuchi	1,982	15.	Mt. Nantai	2,484
5.	Mt. Daisen	1,729	16.	Mt. Zaō	1,841
6.	Mt. Ohminé	1,915	17.	Mt. Iwaté	2,038
7.	Mt. Hakuba	2,932	18.	Mt. Usu	732
8.	Mt. Hodaka	3,190	19.	Mt. Yōtei	1,898
9.	Mt. Ontaké	3,067	20.	Mt. Hojiri	2,052
10.	Mt. Shirané (Kitadaké)	3,192	21.	Mt. Daisetsu	2,290
11.	Mt. Fuji	3,776			

In the famous movie "Godzilla," the prehistoric monster Godzilla vanishes into the crater of Mt. *Mihara.*

Mt. Fuji
The scenic symbol of Japan — this dormant volcano is the nation's tallest peak, at 3,776 meters. The elegant Fuji is the traditional target of Japanese faith, referred to from days of old as the "mountain where the gods dwell."

Mt. Mihara
An active volcano on *Izu-Ōshima* Island. A major eruption occurred in October of 1986, with the 10,000 residents forced to evacuate the island.

17

Most of the rivers in Japan flow down from the mountains which comprise the backbone of the nation. Because the distance to the coastlines is short, the flow of these rivers is swift, with the sand and stone carried by the water creating plains of various different configurations near the ocean. Furthermore, the dams of many hydroelectric plants are built at upstream areas to utilize the power of these rapid currents.

Major Rivers and Plains

1. Tokachi River
2. Ishikari River
3. Kitagami River
4. Abukuma River
5. Tone River
6. Fuji River
7. Tenryū River
8. Yodo River
9. Yoshino River
10. Mogami River
11. Shinano River
12. Kiso River
13. Chikugo River

A. Teshio Plain
B. Tokachi Plain
C. Ishikari Plain
D. Sendai Plain
E. Kantō Plain
F. Nōbi Plain
G. Isé Plain
H. Ōsaka Plain

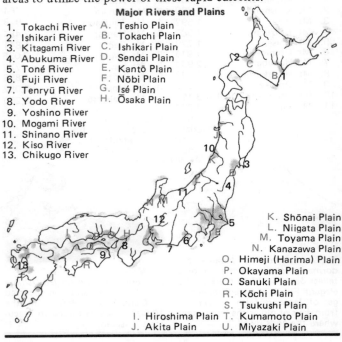

K. Shōnai Plain
L. Niigata Plain
M. Toyama Plain
N. Kanazawa Plain
O. Himeji (Harima) Plain
P. Okayama Plain
Q. Sanuki Plain
R. Kōchi Plain
S. Tsukushi Plain
T. Kumamoto Plain
U. Miyazaki Plain
I. Hiroshima Plain
J. Akita Plain

The short length and swift flow of Japanese rivers has helped generate many distinctive geographical features (notably plains).

Alluvial Fan

The *Jinzū* River in *Toyama* Prefecature flows down from *Hida* Mountain Range to the plain below, where the current picks up speed. Small stones and other debris carried from upstream accumulate at the end of the valley, creating a typical alluvial fan configuration.

Mizuya — an evacuation hut designed for use during floods.

Delta

The flow of the *Ōta* River, which passes through *Hiroshima* City, becomes the most gentle at the spot where it empties into the *Seto* Inland Sea, with the accumulated earth and sand forming a land mass. Modern-day *Hiroshima* City was first established on the delta area created by the flow of the *Ōta* River.

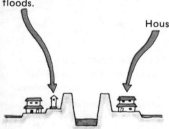

Houses are built on banked up land areas.

Wajū (Dike-Protected Settlement)

The area near the border of *Aichi* and *Mié* prefectures is where the *Kiso, Nagara* and *Ibi* rivers converge. Here, these rivers branch off and empty into the sea, and as a result, this area has been traditionally struck by frequent flood damage. The people living in this region protect their homes and fields from floods by erecting high dikes around the critical points.

Wajū

Japan's mountain ranges and volcanic zones, and the swift waterfall-like rivers which flow between them, have created many distinctive lakes. The Japanese coastal line is also extremely complex, and has a total distance of 29,000 km, or about 75% of the length around the earth at the equator.

The flow attaches here, forming a new course for the river.

The remains of the former river course.

Crescent Moon Lake

The *Ishikari* River in *Hokkaidō* zigzags across the flat *Ishikari* Plain. During floods, the water breaks through the bends in the river curve to form separate flows, leaving the former zigzag course behind to form a crescent moon-shaped lake.

The Layout of *Fuji Goko*
(Fuji Five Lakes)

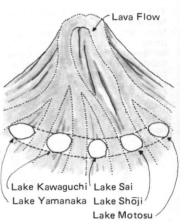

Lava Flow

Lake Kawaguchi　Lake Sai
Lake Yamanaka　Lake Shōji
Lake Motosu

Naturally Dammed Lake

In ancient times, the "Fuji Five Lakes" at the base of Mt. Fuji were a single huge lake. Subsequent eruptions of the volcano resulted in the current five lake formation.

Rias Coast

The *Sanriku* Coast in *Iwaté* Prefecture is a seacoast along which the mountains crowd down close to the water. This is an intricate and heavily used coastline, where a large number of excellent natural harbors have been built. The many tiny inlets and islands which dot the offshore area offer a scenic beauty distinct to the Japanese archipelago. The rias (jagged) coastline of *Matsushima* is regarded as one of the three most scenic places in Japan.

Sanriku Coast

Layout of *Notsuké* Cape in *Hokkaidō*

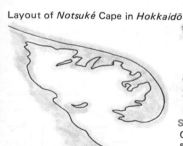

Ama-no-Hashidaté

Sandspits and Sandbars

On complex-shaped coastlines, sand and stone accumulate at the mouth of inlets and other areas behind the flow. The belt-shaped strips of land formed by this process are known as *sashi* (sandspits). When these projections connect with the shore on the other side they become *sasu* (sandbars).

One of Japan's most famous sandspits is Cape *Notsuké* in *Hokkaidō*. Among sandbars, meanwhile, *Ama-no-Hashidaté* in *Kyōto* Prefecture has been designated as one of Japan's three most scenic places.

21

THE CLIMATE OF JAPAN

日本の気候

Japan lies in the northern hemisphere, with the majority of the island chain belonging to temperate zones. However, because of the complex geography and long north-south range, the climate differs broadly by region, even during the same season.

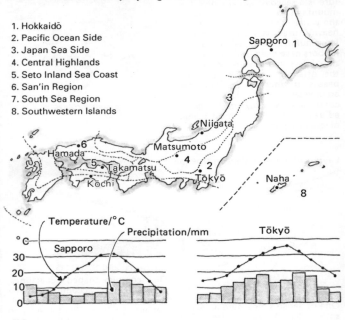

1. Hokkaidō
2. Pacific Ocean Side
3. Japan Sea Side
4. Central Highlands
5. Seto Inland Sea Coast
6. San'in Region
7. South Sea Region
8. Southwestern Islands

Hokkaidō

The main northern island, distinguished by frigid winters, cool summers, and no rainy season.

Pacific Ocean Side

Summers are hot and muggy, while winters are sunny and dry.

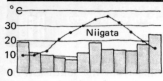

Japan Sea Side

The seasonal winds blowing in from Siberia are moistened by the warm currents of the Japan Sea. These winds then collide with the mountains in central *Honshū*, making this one of the heaviest snowfall regions in the world.

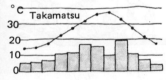

Seto Inland Sea Coast

This region is sandwiched between mountains on the north and south, minimizing the impact of seasonal winds, and ensuring sunny and dry weather throughout the year.

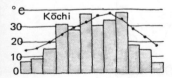

South Sea Region

A region distinguished by warm and rainy weather around the year, a long rainy season, and frequent typhoons.

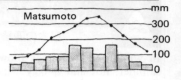

Central Highlands

The region focused on the mountains in central *Honshū* and the basin formed between these mountains. Characterized by wide temperature fluctuations throughout the year and during single days.

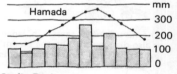

San'in Region

The region most strongly hit by the impact of seasonal winds from Siberia after the Japan sea side of Japan. The weather in winter is perennially cloudy, while summers are hot.

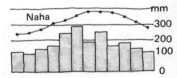

Southwestern Islands

A region with a warm and rainy subtropical climate. The warmest area in Japan, these islands are known for their coconut and mangrove trees.

23

In winter, chilly winds blow from the northwest, while in summer, hot and muggy winds come from the southeast. In the spring and autumn these seasonal winds (also known as "monsoons") fluctuate widely. *Haru-Ichiban* refers to the first strong southeast wind of the year, which blows as the season shifts from winter to spring.

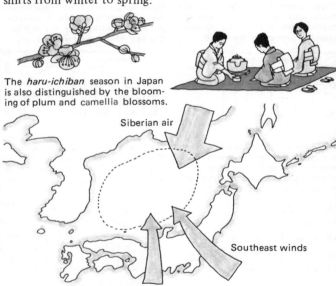

The *haru-ichiban* season in Japan is also distinguished by the blooming of plum and camellia blossoms.

Siberian air

Southeast winds

In winter the powerful Siberian air mass gradually weakens, with low pressure fronts finally reach Japan. Around that time, strong and warm southeast winds serve to carry in these low pressure masses. These winds are known as *haru-ichiban,* and the sharp temperature rise often triggers avalanches in heavy snowfall regions.

To the Japanese, the blooming of the cherry blossoms signals the end of another long winter, and the arrival of spring. The "cherry blossom front" refers to a theoretical line connecting the first blooming of these blossoms from region to region. The front travels north from Okinawa to Hokkaidō, providing a barometer of the official arrival of spring from late March to mid-May.

Hanami (Flower-viewing)

Around the time that cherry blossoms come into full bloom, picnic-like parties are held under the trees to view the flowers. This custom is known as *hanami* (flower viewing). In past ages this was one of the many events used to celebrate the arrival of spring. More recently, however, it has come to be utilized as one of the limited opportunities to hold outdoor drinking parties.

May 10

April 30

April 20

April 10

March 30

Sakura Zensen (Cherry Blossom Front)

The line linking the initial days of bloom of cherry trees in the various different regions.

Hanami: vol. 1 p.85/vol. 2 p.101, p.154/vol.8 p.99

With the exception of *Hokkaidō*, rainy weather continues throughout Japan for about one month from mid-June. This phenomenon is caused by the collision above the island chain of cold winds blowing from the Okhotsk Sea and warm winds from the South Pacific, generating rain clouds. When the ensuing rainy season comes to an end, summer has truly arrived.

Cold winds from the Okhotsk Sea

Rainy season front

Warm winds from the Pacific Ocean

This is also the season in which torrential downpours often result in flood damage.

This is a very pleasant season in *Hokkaidō*, with many travelers making their way to the large northern isle.

Late August through September is the typhoon season in Japan. With rice crops generally ripening in September, typhoons have been one of the greatest threats to the Japanese lifestyle since ancient times.

Major Typhoons in Recent Years — Routes and Damage

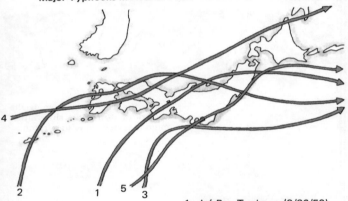

Widely known as days in which typhoons traditionally strike are the 210th and 220th days after the official first day of spring.

1. Isé Bay Typhoon (9/26/59): 4,700 killed, 401 missing, 38,917 injured.
2. Makurazaki Typhoon (9/17/45): 2,483 killed, 1,283 missing, 2,452 injured.
3. Typhoon Catheline (9/15/47): 1,041 killed, 488 missing, 1,841 injured.
4. Tōyamaru Typhoon (9/26/54): 1,327 killed, 371 missing, 1,378 injured.
5. Kanogawa Typhoon (9/26/58): 874 killed, 283 missing, 1,849 injured.

September is known for the *akisamé zensen* (autumn rain front), and the number of rainy days increases, much like the early summer rainy season *(Tsuyu)*. This front fades in October, marking the arrival of the most pleasant season of the year in Japan.

While the cherry blossom is the symbol of spring, the chrysanthemum is associated with autumn.

Famous areas for viewing the changing of the leaves in autumn include *Oirasé* River in *Aomori* Prefecture, and the *Arashiyama* area of *Kyōto.*

This is by far the most pleasant season during which to travel in Japan, and the areas known for their beautiful colors are visited by considerable crowds.

Toward the latter half of October Siberian air masses are generated, and chilly winds known as *kogarashi* (winds which wither trees) herald the full-fledged arrival of winter. In the heavy snowfall seasons of *Hokkaidō* and the Japan Sea side of the nation, the fierce battle with winter begins.

When snow accumulates, Japanese children, like children everywhere, built snowmen, have snowball fights, and frolic in other ways.

In the past, children in the "snow country" regions built *Kamakura* (igloo-like snow huts), and played inside.

In contrast, on the Pacific Ocean side sunny days are the rule. During a rare blizzard in *Tōkyō*, in only two days more than 800 people sustained broken bones and other injuries from slipping and falling in the snow.

Kamakura: vol. 4 p.26

DISASTERS
災害

Japan is a nation in which 67% of the land is covered with forests, while containing 200 or more volcanoes, complex geographical features, and violent climatical changes. In short, it is an environment heavily prone to disasters. In a sense, the history of Japan represents a sustained battle with natural calamity.

There is an old saying that children are most afraid of "earthquakes, lightning, fires, and the father". In recent years, however, there has been a definite decrease in the number of children who fear their dad.

Earthquakes

At 5:46 AM on January 17, 1995, an earthquake of magnitude 7.2 struck southern Hyōgo prefecture and western Ōsaka. This earthquake, known as the Great Hanshin Earthquake of 1995, killed 6,300 persons and injured another 43,000. In addition, a total of 436,000 homes were destroyed. It was Japan's worst natural disaster since the end of WWII.

Storm and Flood Damage

The damage which occurs during typhoons or large storms during the rainy season. Major property losses often result from flooding or high tides.

Snow Damage

Mounting countermeasures against avalanches and other snow-related damage is a major lifestyle theme in the heavy snowfall regions of the Japan Sea side of the nation.

Landslides

Japan has many regions with weak foundations, in which landslides can be triggered by heavy rains, earthquakes, and other phenomena.

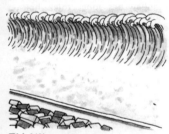

Tidal Waves (Tsunami)

A nation surrounded on all sides by ocean, Japan has been known to sustain damage even from tidal waves generated by earthquakes in distant places. Following the great Chile earthquake of 1960, for example, over 1,000 Japanese were killed or injured by the ensuing tidal wave which reached nation's shores.

Volcanic Eruptions

Not only do volcanic eruptions take their toll in human life, the lava flows destroy homes and fields, while volcanic ash can obliterate agricultural crops. There are some people who say that the 1986 eruption of Mt. *Mihara* is a warning that Mt. *Fuji* is next on the list.

日本の天然記念物

Mammals

Kamoshika (Mountain goat)

Standing about 1 - 1.5 meters high, the *kamoshika* resembles a goat, and has two single-prong black horns. With its fur highly valued for its rarity, poaching has forced this species to the brink of extinction.

Nihonzaru (Japanese macaque monkey)

About 50 - 70 cm in height, this monkey has long, thick hair, a short tail, and red face and rear end. The species is well known for its highly organized social structure, with a so-called "boss" monkey at the top.

Iriomoté wild cat

A rare mammal discovered in 1965, and said to be the closest living species to the ancestor of the common cat.

Amami hare

A primeval-appearing rabbit, referred to many as a "living fossil."

Toki (Japanese Crested Ibis)

The pale red pattern on its feathers and graceful proportions make the *toki* a truly exquisite bird. Unfortunately, it is nearing extinction, with only a bird known to be alive in captivity.

Onagadori (Long-tailed cock)

A type of chicken dating from the Edo period. A result of mutation, the tail feathers of the male grow to abnormal lengths, sometimes as long as 12 m.

Raichō (Snow grouse)

A bird which inhabits alpine regions. In order to gain protection from predators, its wing color changes by season — to white in the winter, and a brownish tone in the summer.

Tanchōzuru (Japanese crane)

The most beautiful of all Japanese crane species, the *tanchōzuru* has been loved from times of old as a symbol of long life, love and elegance.

Amphibians and Insects

Ōsanshō-uo (Cryptobranchoidea)
One of the largest amphibians in the world today, with specimens over one meter in length having been recorded.

Kabutogani (Helmet crab)
A type of arthropod about 60 cm in length. In its larval stage, this crab resembles the now extinct trilobite.

Plants

Yaku Sugi (Kagoshima pref.)
A jumbo-size cedar tree growing in the primeval forests of the Miyanouradaké hills. With a maximum root circumference of 43 m and a height of 30 m, some of these trees are said to be over 7,000 years in age.

Ozé Mizubashō (Gumma pref.)
The Ozé region is one of the most humid areas in Japan, and is particularly famous for its huge fields of *mizubashō* (skunk cabbage).

THE LIFESTYLE
OF
THE JAPANESE

•

日本人の生活

OVERVIEW

Over five decades have elapsed since Japan's crushing defeat in World War II. Rising with incredible speed from the ashes of war to achieve unparalleled social restoration, the nation has passed through the age of accelerated economic growth of the 1960s, and the two separate oil crises of the 1970s. In the 1990s, Japan has truly attained the status of an economic superpower, and the lifestyles of the Japanese have undergone sweeping changes as a result.

One of the most distinguishing characteristics of present-day Japanese society is the comparatively small gaps in wealth. Statistics show that over 90% of the Japanese consider themselves members of the "middle class." Few if any seriously consider themselves "upper class" (rich) or "lower class" (poor).

Another key point in examining the Japanese life-style is to recognize the situation related to land. Japan is a small nation in terms of area, and with the population now heavily concentrated in the cramped plain areas (and particularly big cities), the price of land has skyrocketed. It is quite normal, for example, for a home in central Tōkyō to be worth one billion yen. As a result, the majority of businessmen are forced to live in the suburbs, with commuting time of two hours or more now common place.

In the 50 odd years following World War II, Japan has risen to claim a firm position in the global order. In these times, the question of how to make the lifestyle of individual Japanese truly affluent in the genuine sense of the word is being asked with greater frequency than ever before.

POPULATION TRENDS AND DISTRIBUTION

人口

The population of Japan has reached the 126 million mark, about triple the level in 1900. Projections call for a peak of 128 million to be attained around the year 2010, followed by a gradual decline due to a subsequent decrease in the birth rate. In 2050, the population is expected to be about 100.5 million.

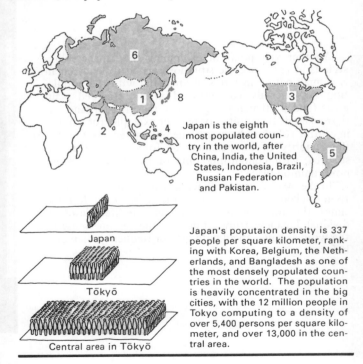

Japan is the eighth most populated country in the world, after China, India, the United States, Indonesia, Brazil, Russian Federation and Pakistan.

Japan

Tōkyō

Central area in Tōkyō

Japan's poputaion density is 337 people per square kilometer, ranking with Korea, Belgium, the Netherlands, and Bangladesh as one of the most densely populated countries in the world. The population is heavily concentrated in the big cities, with the 12 million people in Tokyo computing to a density of over 5,400 persons per square kilometer, and over 13,000 in the central area.

The average life span in Japan is 84 years for women and 77 years for men, ranking the Japanese among the Swedish, Swiss, and Norwegians as one of the longest living peoples on earth. This expanded longevity has translated into an increase in the number of Japanese elderly, with welfare programs for these senior citizens now looming as a major political issue in Japan.

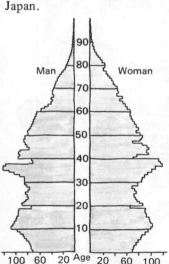

Unit/ Ten thousand people

Population Phyramid by Age Group

As shown, the next decade will bring a sharp increase in the number of elderly, heralding the arrival of a genuine aged society in Japan.

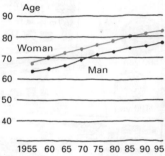

Trends in the Average Life Span

Through the 1930s, a Japanese could expect to live for an average of 50 years. The next three decades were marked by a remarkable increase in longevity, with Japan entering the ranks of long-living world populaces in the 1960s. This progress underscores vast improvements made in the level of the Japanese diet and medical care, achieved on the strength of the nation's dynamic postwar reconstruction and accelerated economic growth.

The Bank of Japan now issues three types of banknotes and six types of coins. Credit cards are also gaining in popularity, making it easier to make purchases without carrying around excessive cash.

10,000 yen

500 yen

100 yen

50 yen

5,000 yen

10 yen

2,000 yen

5 yen

1,000 yen

1 yen

One yen and five yen coins are not widely used. Ten yen and 100 yen coins are used mostly in pay phones or vending machines, and carrying a reasonable amount of them around is a good idea.

Foreign currency or travelers checks may be exchanged for Japanese yen at banks with exchange counters. All city banks (banks with branches on a nationwide basis) conduct foreign exchange operations, although many of the small- to medium-size banks or regional branches do not operate such counters.

American Express, VISA, Mastercard and other credit cards may be used in Japan as well. There are also various other types of credit cards which are issued for domestic use.

Establishments generally display the types of credit cards which they accept.

Credit cards may be used at most department stores, hotels and larger restaurants. At coffee shops, pubs, grocery stores and other smaller scale restaurants and stores, however, cash is the general rule.

LIFE IN THE BIG CITY

都市の暮らし

Roughly 10% of the Japanese population, or 12 million people, live in Tōkyō, one of the world's largest cities. As a result, life in Tōkyō is considerably different from the cities of other regions. Here, we use the example of an average Japanese businessman to introduce life in Tōkyō.

The majority of people dwelling in the greater Tōkyō area are originally from other parts of Japan, with most households consisting of small-scale nuclear families (husband, wife and one or two children).

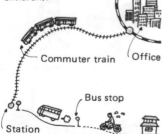

The average commuting time for a Tōkyō businessman is about 90 minutes (one way). Because of the extremely high price of land in central Tōkyō, families are forced retreat to the suburbs to realize satisfactory lifestyles.

On the other side of the coin are landowners in central Tōkyō, who, when they sell their property, literally become millionaires overnight.

Commuting Rush

Because the majority of businessman commute into Tōkyō from the suburbs, the morning and evening rush hours are deadly to say the least. As a result, most businessmen expend much of their energy just getting to work.

Entertainment Districts

Tōkyō contains several large entertainment districts, which offer a wealth of amusement facilities to choose from. Businessmen often use these areas to relieve their stress.

Fads

Tōkyō is also the source of new fads and trends sparked by young people. In no time at all, these fads spread to other regions, causing the young people in the prefectures to develop a strong fascination with the capital.

Solo Assignment (Tanshin Funin)

To most businessmen in large companies, transfers are an inevitable fate and duty. With the strong concern for education in Japan, many husbands choose to live alone during their assignments overseas or in other prefectures, to avoid forcing their children to change schools. These households experience various problems rooted to this "separated" format lifestyle.

LIFE ON THE FARM
農村の暮らし

There are fewer and fewer truly "full-time farmers" left in modern-day Japan. In most rural households, several family members are engaged in work other than farming, while all of these communities are now plagued by an exodus of young people to the big cities.

Most farming households consist of extended families, with the parents and children living under the same roof as the grandparents. This is the traditional Japanese lifestyle pattern, although the nation's rapid urbanization has caused major changes in family structure.

With the steady stream of people into the cities, some country houses are deserted. In recent years, many urban dwellers are leaving the city to dwell in these houses and launch their own rural lifestyles.

44

Among "side-business farms," the father is often engaged in work other than agriculture. There is a vast number of such households in Japan today, with the grandparents and wife acting as the principal farmers.

Public transportation is limited in regional areas, and automobiles are the principal means of getting around. Because each working family member needs a car to commute, some rural households must purchase and maintain as many as four to five vehicles.

Rural towns offered rather limited recreation, making festivals one of the major enjoyments of the citizens. There are two major types of festivals in farming communities — those held in the spring to pray for rich crops, and those held in the autumn to thank the gods for the harvest.

During *Shōgatsu* (New Year's) and *Bon* (the Buddhist holiday in mid-August when the spirits of departed ancestors are believed to return), city dwellers return to their traditional family homes. At these times, the normally lonely and deserted farming communities suddenly bustle with activity.

THE LIFE OF A CITY DWELLER 都市生活者の一生

Childhood Years

With the father away at work and rarely home, city children tend to spend most of their time with their mother. In homes in which both parents work, some children must look after the house until either the father or mother comes home.

Big cities are full of paved roads and have few parks, depriving children of the opportunity to play in nature. As a result, video games and other indoor amusements are popular.

THE LIFE OF A SUBURBAN DWELLER 農村生活者の一生

Childhood Years

Because the parents in a side-job farming household are extremely busy, the children are normally raised by the grandparents. When there is a large number of children, raising them becomes the work of the family unit as a whole, with youngsters coming into contact with many different adults from an early age on.

In farming communities located in a rich natural environment, the children swim in rivers, collect insects, and dream up other amusements on their own. Few will stay closed up indoors.

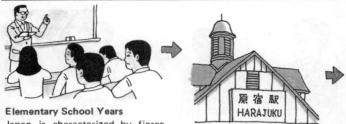

Elementary School Years

Japan is characterized by fierce school entrance examination competition, and in the big cities getting one's children into a famous private junior high school is considered the first step to future success. To achieve this objective, elementary school children must spend long hours studying in *juku* (cram schools) even after their regular school classes are over.

Junior High School Years

Around this time, Tōkyō junior high school students begin to seek out amusement in *Harajuku, Shinjuku* and other youthful entertainment districts.

Elementary School Years

Television now immediately carries city fads to the children of the countryside. Those who have played mostly outdoors begin to develop an interest in video games and other amusements at this age.

Junior High School Years

The greatest pleasure to the countrified junior high school students of farming communities is sports. When classes let out, most of them participate in baseball practice or other team or club activities until evening.

High School Years

Graduating from a top-class university is a prerequisite for entering a top-class company, and high school students are forced to study hard for the entrance exams. High school students who are not concerned with these exams, meanwhile, spend less time hitting the books.

College Years

After arising victorious from the entrance exam wars, for most Japanese college students these years are the most carefree period of their lives. College students attend classes in their spare time, spending most of their effort dating, playing sports, or working at part-time jobs.

Many young people from the country enter city universities, and join the ranks of urban dwellers.

High School Years

The high school students of rural areas have a burning fascination with big cities, and particularly Tōkyō. One of their biggest dreams is to dress up in the latest fashions and take a pleasure trip to Tōkyō.

High school students who do not go on to college find jobs close to their family home.

Employment

Japanese businessmen rarely change jobs, meaning that the company they first enter will largely determine the rest of their lives. Because of this, one's first job is considered the most important crossroads in life.

Those who tire of life on the farm sometimes quit their local jobs to seek out work in the cities.

Young people who remain in the country must help out with the farm work at home. Most end up spending their entire lives in these communities, eventually taking over the family farm from their parents.

Marriage

Supporting a family in the big cities, where the prices of land and commodities are exorbitant, requires considerable income. This has caused a gradual increase in the age at which Japanese businessmen marry, while there are more and more families in which both parents hold down jobs.

Marriage

The biggest problem in rural communities is the shortage of eligible young women. Almost all go off to study or work in the cities, greatly reducing the possibilities of young farmers meeting up with the girl of their dreams. Some communities tackle this problem by inviting groups of city girls to participate in prospective marriage parties.

Employment: vol. 8 p.32 **Working couples:** vol. 8 p.109

Childbirth

The higher standard of living and greater emphasis on private time has seen a steady decrease in the birth rate in Japan. In the big cities, there is an increasing number of couples who are choosing not to have child.

Work

The work habits of the Japanese businessman continue to be awesome. Overtime until late at night and reporting to work on holidays are still considered natural customs at many companies.

Childbirth

Farming communities continue to retain a deep-rooted sense of "the more children the better," and the birth rate is comparatively high as a result. Giving birth to a son who will take over the family business is considered a particularly important duty for women who marry into farming households.

Work

Japan is a country with limited land space, making it extremely difficult to raise a family through farming alone. As a result, most men in the prime of life work at companies. In the snow country, meanwhile, many husbands travel to the big cities to work as seasonal laborers during the winter months (when farming is impossible).

See vol. 8 chapter 3 "The work of Salaryman".

Retirement

For businessmen who place work before their private lives, mandatory retirement can provide quite a shock. Many Japanese use retirement as an opportunity to begin a totally new lifestyle.

> In recent years, some people who have wearied of city life are moving to the country to begin new careers as farmers.

Retirement

As long as there is land, there will be no such thing as "retirement" on the farm. In fact, the exodus of young people to the cities has caused men in the prime of life to take jobs other than farming to supplement their income, with the actual farm work now increasingly performed by the elderly.

Elderly Years

More elderly Japanese are choosing to spend their autumn years in fancy retirement homes or overseas resort facilities. On the other hand, a social problem has surfaced in which an increasing number of senior citizens dwell separately from their children, passing lonely autumn years in big city apartments.

Elderly Years

The primary responsibility of elderly people on the farm is to take care of their grandchildren. However, as the children leave home, many older couples find themselves living lonely lives in huge country houses.

Retirement: vol. 8 p.54   **Growing Old:** vol.17 p.30

特色ある地方

The regions of Japan offer various distinguishing characteristics rooted in the wide range of climates and geography. Furthermore, the people of these areas have created their own unique cultures and lifestyle patterns. In this section, we examine a few of these regions.

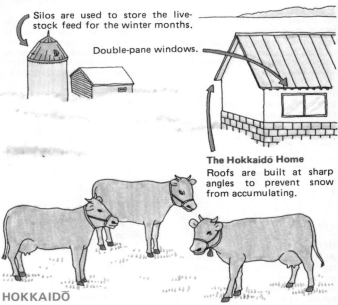

Silos are used to store the livestock feed for the winter months.

Double-pane windows.

The Hokkaidō Home
Roofs are built at sharp angles to prevent snow from accumulating.

HOKKAIDŌ

Hokkaidō is the major northern isle of Japan, where temperatures drop to as low as minus 30 degrees centigrade at the height of winter. Utilizing the vast pasture areas of the island, *Hokkaidō* is the site of large-scale dairy farming — a genuine rarity in the rest of Japan.

THE SNOW COUNTRY

The Japan Sea side of the nation is one of the world's premiere heavy snowfall regions. Battling snow which accumulates to depths of three to four meters is a critical aspect of the lifestyles of people in this area.

Snow-Melting Roads

In *Nagaoka* City in *Niigata* Prefecture, water pipes are built beneath the roads, with a continuous spray issued to melt the snow on the pavement surface.

Tsukemono (Pickled Vegetables)

Transportation is anything but convenient during the long winter season, making it difficult to obtain fresh foods. The people of this region respond by preserving cabbage, cucumbers and other vegetables through pickling.

Yukioroshi (Snow Clearing)

By far the most back-breaking work in the snow country is clearing accumulated snow from roofs. In regions where the snow piles up to depths of two meters or more, if this shoveling work is not performed at least five times during the winter, the roof may buckle under the sheer weight of the snow.

MOUNTAIN VILLAGES

With some 67% of Japan's land covered with wooded areas, the forestry industry has flourished from days of old. However, the industry is now being hit hard by the steady shift from wood to new materials for home building, large volume imports of cheap foreign lumber and other developments, with sweeping lifestyle changes having come to Japan's mountain villages.

In the past, freshly cut logs were hauled down from mountains through following method:

The cut logs were immediately stripped of their bark, and dropped into a gorge.

From there, horses were used to haul the logs to a river.

A log raft was formed, and floated to a downstream port.

Today, excellent logging roads enable trucks to replace rafts as the means of carrying timber to market.

HIGHLANDS

The highlands zone running along central *Honshū* has an average temperature of 20 degrees C even in the summer, and often reaches levels as low as minus 20 degrees in winter. This cool climate is utilized for large-scale vegetable cultivation and other agriculture.

The highlands are plagued by fog in the morning and night, which often blocks the sunlight and interferes with crop growth.

The soil is formed from the lava of past volcanic eruptions and the volcanic ash which has settled on top of that. As a result, it is low in nutrients, and does not lend itself to rice growing.

The local farmers have reacted by growing cauliflower, cabbage, lettuce, and other vegetables which can be cultivated in cooler climates.

These vegetables are now shipped to various areas of Japan, with the focus on the Tōkyō and Ōsaka regions.

SHIRASU DAICHI (WHITE SAND TABLELANDS)

The word *shirasu* means "white sand," and refers to volcanic ash sand which contains large amounts of quartz, andesite and other types of rock. About 60% of the soil in the heavily volcanic region of *Kagoshima* Prefecture consists of this white sand, and the lack of water has forced the local farmers to truly struggle to develop the land and raise successful crops.

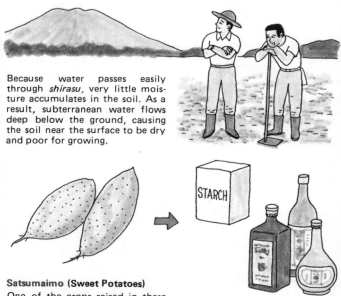

Because water passes easily through *shirasu*, very little moisture accumulates in the soil. As a result, subterranean water flows deep below the ground, causing the soil near the surface to be dry and poor for growing.

STARCH

Satsumaimo (Sweet Potatoes)

One of the crops raised in these *shirasu* tablelands is the sweet potato, brought to *Kagoshima* from *Okinawa* about 260 years ago. The hard work of the local farmers has resulted in 30% of all sweet potatoes in Japan being supplied from *Kagoshima*.

Some 70% of the sweet potatoes grown in *Kagoshima* Prefecture are processed into starch, and are also used to produce *shōchū* (a liquor distilled from sweet potatoes), starch syrup and other foodstuffs.

ISLANDS

In addition to the four main isles of *Hokkaidō, Honshū, Shikoku* and *Kyūshū* (from north to south), Japan also contains several thousand smaller islands. The livelihood of the people who dwell on these islands is focused on fishing, and they tend to preserve their own unique lifestyle patterns and culture as a result.

The majority of island fishing is concentrated on sardines, mackerel, sea bream and other coastal varieties, with the people continuing to fish in small boats with poles.

Most of the farming land on the smaller islands is characterized by steep inclines and cramped size. In addition, the poor quality of the soil also helps make these regions less than ideal for rice growing. The pattern is to turn these areas into pasture land, and raise cattle, wheat, millet and other livestock and crops.

Sado and other remote islands were formerly inhabited by social exiles or prisoners, and many remains of tragic generals, religious leaders, or other historical figures can be found there.

Many of the subtropical zone southwest islands and the islands close to the big cities on the Pacific Ocean side of Japan serve as resort meccas for young people in the summer.

- January 1: *Shōgatsu*
  New Year's Day
- The Second Monday in Jan:
  Seijin-no-hi Adult's Day
- February 3: *Setsubun*
  Last Day of Winter
- February 11 : *Kenkoku Kinembi*
  National Foundation Day
- March 3: *Hinamatsuri*
  Girl's Festival
- March 21 : *Shumbun-no-hi*
  Vernal Equinox
- April 29: *Midori-no-hi*
  The Greenery Day
- May 3 : *Kempō Kinembi*
  Constitution Day
- May 4: *Kokumin-no kyūjitsu*
  People's Holiday
- May 5: *Kodomo-no-hi*
  Children's Day
- July 7: *Tanabata*
  Star Festival (Held on August 7 in some regions)
- July 20: *Umi-no-hi* Marine Day
- Mid-August: *Bon* All Soul's Day
- Mid-September: *Tsukimi*
  Moon Viewing
- September 15: *Keirō-no-hi*
  Respect for the Aged Day
- September 23: *Shūbun-no-hi*
  Autumnal Equinox
- The Second Monday in Oct:
  Taiiku-no-hi Sport's Day
- November 3: *Bunka-no-hi*
  Culture Day
- November 23: *Kinrō Kansha-no-hi*
  Labor Thanksgiving Day
- December 23: *Tennō Tanjōbi*
  The Emperor's Birthday
- December 31: *Ō-misoka*
  New Year's Eve

● = National holiday

SHŌGATSU (NEW YEAR'S)

Shōgatsu is the most important day of the year for most Japanese. People participant in various types of events and activities, and pray for good luck during the upcoming year.

Hatsuhinodé (New Year's Day Sunrise)

According to the ancient Japanese religion of *Shintō*, the sun is the most important god in the univers. From this was born the belief that praying to the morning sun on January 1 will bring good fortune and happiness throughout the new year.

Hatsumōdé (First Shrine Visit of the Year)

After the clock strikes midnight on January 1, people gather at shrines to pray for a healthy and fruitful new year.

Shishimai (Lion Dance)

A man wearing a Chinese lion mask dances in front of neighborhood homes, to the tune of a flute and hand drum. It is believed that this dance drives away all evil spirits, and protects the health of the people of the community.

Shōgatsu Dishes

Often used in *Osechi-ryōri* are boiled fish paste *(kamaboko)*, shrimp and other marine products, as well as various types of vegetables.

Zōni (Rice Cakes and Vegetables)

Zōni, a boiled soup made with rice cakes, radish and other vegetables, is the single most popular food eaten at *Shōgatsu*. The Japanese believe that eating *zōni* will guarantee a long and healthy life.

Osechi-ryōri (New Year Dishes)

Osechi-ryōri features various types of dishes prepared exclusively for New Year's, packed into special tiered lacquered boxes. These dishes are generally prepared to be preserved for several days, to help liberate housewives from some of their housework duties during this hectic holiday season.

Shōgatsu Amusements

Takoagé (Kite Flying)

Hanetsuki (Japanese-Style Badminton)

The losers may have their faces painted with charcoal.

Koma (Spinning Top)

During *Shōgatsu*, children receive *otoshidama* (gifts of money) from their parents and relatives.

SETSUBUN (THE END OF WINTER)

Setsubun is February 3, and is observed as the day when winter ends and spring begins. The main event of this day is the throwing of roasted soybeans in homes and offices, to drive out any evil spirits *(oni)* lurking on the premises.

On this day everyone is supposed to eat as many beans as they are years old.

These beans are tossed throughout the house, repeating the chant *Oni wa soto, fuku wa uchi* ("Devils be banished, happiness remain").

Men dressed as devils will often perform a dance.

Shrines or temples often hold gatherings to throw *fuku-mamé* (lucky beans) or *fuku-mochi* (lucky rice cakes) over the assembled throngs. Catching and eating these beans and cakes is thought to bring good luck.

HINAMATSURI (GIRL'S FESTIVAL)

The "Girl's Festival" on March 3, also known as the "Peach Tree Festival," is held to pray for the happiness of female children. On this day, households with young girls display beautiful doll sets, drink *shiro-zaké* (white *saké* brewed from *saké* and rice malt), and offer *hishi-mochi* lozenge-shaped rice cakes).

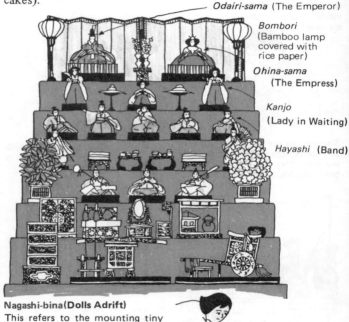

Odairi-sama (The Emperor)

Bombori (Bamboo lamp covered with rice paper)

Ohina-sama (The Empress)

Kanjo (Lady in Waiting)

Hayashi (Band)

Nagashi-bina (Dolls Adrift)

This refers to the mounting tiny dolls in miniature boats, which are then set adrift down a river. It is believed that dolls will carry away all misery and hardship on their trip.

KODOMO-NO-HI (CHILDREN'S DAY)

Children's Day on May 5, also known as "Boy's Festival," is held to pray for the health and success of male children. On this day, households with young boys hang out *koinobori* (carp streamers) and decorate their homes with "May dolls."

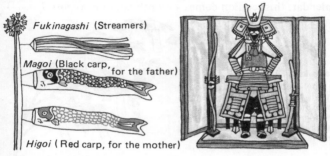

Fukinagashi (Streamers)

Magoi (Black carp, for the father)

Higoi (Red carp, for the mother)

Koinobori (Carp Streamers)

In Japan, the carp has a reputation as a fish with a tremendous will to live, capable of swimming up and over fierce flowing waterfalls.

Gogatsu-ningyō (May Dolls)

Also known as *Musha (samurai)* dolls, these dolls are attired in traditional military armor, and incorporate the wish that the boys grow up to be as strong as *samurai* warriors.

"Golden Week"

With three national holidays falling close together on the calendar (The Greenery Day on April 29, Constitution Day on May 3 and Children's Day on May 5), this period is known as "Golden Week" and is utilized as a major spring vacation season in Japan.

TANABATA (STAR FESTIVAL)

According to Chinese folklore, *Kengyū* (the Cowherd or Altair) and *Shokujo* (the Weaver Princess or Vega), a pair of lovers separated by the Milky Way, are able to cross the stars and renew their love once each year — on July 7. On the lunar calendar, this reunion comes a month later on August 7.

Tanzaku

It is believed that wishes will come true when they are written on these *tanzaku* (paper strips for writing *tanka* or *haiku* poetry), then tied to bamboo tree branches on the day of *Tanabata*.

Tsukimi (Moon Viewing)

Moon-viewing parties are traditionally held on the night of the full moon in mid-September. This moon is also known as the *jūgoya* (equivalent of "harvest moon"), and is considered the most beautiful full moon of the year.

Aki no Nanakusa
(The seven autumn flowers)

Susuki (Pampas grass)

The Japanese see the image of a rabbit pounding a rice cake in the face of the moon.

Tsukimi Dango (Cold dumpling type sweets enjoyed during moon viewing)

BON (ALL SOUL'S DAY)

Bon is the Japanese translation for the Sanskrit "Ulambana," a word with the original meaning of "terrible affliction." In Japan, *Bon* is celebrated as the day when the spirits of departed ancestors return, with various activities held to provide a warm welcome.

Bon Odori (Bon Dancing)

A ritual dance held to welcome back the spirits of the dead. People wear lightweight cotton gowns *(yukata)*, form a circle and dance to the rhythm of festival music known as *hayashi*.

Paying a visit to the ancestral grave is another important part of *Bon*.

Okuribi (Departure Bonfire)

A fire burned to proclaim the departure to the souls of the dead ancestors.

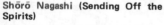

Shōrō Nagashi (Sending Off the Spirits)

In order to return the spirits to the realm of the dead, a light is set burning in a small decorative straw boat, which is then sent off down a river. This custom has largely died out, but is still carried on in some regions.

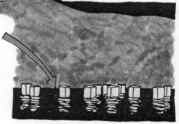

Bon falls on July 15 on the lunar calendar, but today the occasion is normally celebrated according to the solar calendar on August 15.

Bon: vol.4 p.170, p.172/vol.8 p.116/vol.17 p.90

SHICHI-GO-SAN (FESTIVAL FOR 3, 5 AND 7 YEAR OLD'S)

The *Shichi-Go-San* festival on November 15 is held to pray for the health and long life of 3- and 7-year-old girls and 5-year-old boys. The major activity consists of dressing up the children in traditional wear for shrine visits.

Chitosé-amé (Thousand Year Candy)
Chitosé literally means 1,000 years, and *amé* is candy. It is believed that eating this long white stick candy will bring long life, and *chitosé-amé* is widely sold on shrine grounds during *Shichi-Go-San* festival days.

Montsuki Hakama (Crested Ceremonial Clothes) — Formal Japanese-style wear for men.

Furisodé (Long-Sleeve *Kimono*) — Formal Japanese-style wear for unmarried women.

Christmas

While Japan has few real Christians, Christmas itself is celebrated in a gala fashion comparable to America or Europe. Leading up to Christmas Eve, many Japanese decorate their homes or shops with fir tree branches, and on that night eat "Christmas Cake", and bring home presents for the children.

ŌMISOKA (NEW YEAR'S EVE)

December 31 is an extremely busy day for the Japanese, who hustle about preparing for *shōgatsu*, and take part in events geared to banish all bad fortune accumulated over the past 12 months.

Kiné (Pestle): This utensil is used to pound the rice.

Usu (Mortar): The pasty rice is placed in here.

Mochitsuki (Rice-Cake Pounding)

Mochi (rice cakes), the traditional *shōgatsu* dish, was formally made from scratch by individual households. Today, there are still many families in the countryside who carry on this custom.

Seibo (End-of-the-Year Presents)

This refers to the custom of giving presents at the end of the year, to express gratitude to those who have been of service or assistance. An identical present-giving season also occurs during mid-July, and is known as *ochūgen* (mid-year presents).

Joya no Kané (Ringing Out the Old Year)

On New Year's Eve night, the temples around Japan ring their ceremonial bells 108 times. According to the teachings of Buddhism, human beings are plagued by 108 sins, with each ringing of the bell believed to banish a particular fault. When the sound of the final gong fades, the world is renewed, and human beings are free to begin the new year with a clean slate.

The Japanese are originally an agricultural race, with the focus on rice-growing, and have devised many different festivals to go along with their lifestyle. Spring festivals, for example, are held to pray for rich crops, summer festivals seek to protect the rice against drought, pests, typhoons and other disaster, while autumn festivals thank the gods for the successful harvest.

Gion Matsuri (Gion Festival — July 1 - 29, Kyoto)
This festival is said to date from the ninth century, when the citizens of Kyoto organized it as a means to drive out the plague. On July 16 and 17, two dozen elegantly decorated floats are paraded around the city, in a procession which brings the festival to a thrilling climax.

Namahagé (Devil's Mask — December 31, Akita)
Men decked out in straw capes and devil masks make the rounds of the neighborhood, to frighten the children and discourage laziness. This is a custom held to pray for good luck and rich crops throughout the coming year.

Nebuta Festival (August 2 - 7, Aomori)
This is a type of festival originally held to cast sleeping spirits into rivers, in order to drive them out to sea. The Aomori Nebuta Festival is highlighted by huge floats painted with pictures of *samurai* warriors and *kabuki* actors.

See vol. 4 "Festivals of Japan".

Sapporo Yuki Matsuri
(*Sapporo* Snow Festival–early in February, Hokkaidō)
A festival highlighted by spectacular displays of gigantic snow sculptures.

Hakata Gion Yamagasa
(July 1–15, Fukuoka)
Famous for competition in which *"oiyama"* floats are carried around.

Nebuta Festival

Namahagé

Gion Matsuri

Awaodori (Awaodori Dance)— August 12 - 15, Tokushima)
The largest scale *bon-odori* dancing spectacle in Japan.

Hamamatsu Matsuri
(*Hamamatsu* Festival – May 3–5, Shizuoka)
Teams of 165 people cooperate to fly over-sized (three by six meter square) kites.

Kanda Matsuri
(*Kanda* Festival–Mid-May in every other year, Tokyo)
Focused on a procession of jumbo-scale portable shrines (*omikoshi*). The largest festival in Tokyo, held from the *Edo* period on.

69

Weddings and funerals are extremely important occasions in Japan, a society which places great emphasis on blood and community ties. Moreover, attending the weddings or funerals of business colleagues or clients is another key responsibility of Japanese businessmen.

Ceremonial Dress

Hikidemono (Presents given to persons attending a wedding ceremony)

Buddhist rosary beans

Weddings

The general outfit for men is a black formal suit and a white shirt and tie. Overly colorful clothes are frowned upon. Women are expected to attend in a *kimono* or formal dress.

Funerals

Men wear the same black suit and white shirt as they do at weddings, with a black (instead of white) tie. Women wear a black *kimono* or simple black dress. Colorful clothes at a funeral is considered insulting and out of place.

The wedding use *noshibukuro* is tied with red and white string, and usually bears the character *kotobuki* ("congratulations").

Persons attending a wedding or funeral place a certain amount of money inside a special formal envelop *noshibukuro,* and leave it at a special table provided for that purpose. The amount varies according to the relationship with the family or person involved, but generally ranges from 10,000 to 50,000 yen.

The funeral use *noshibukuro* is tied with black and white string, and bears the characters *Goreizen* ("before the spirit of the departed").

Wedding Ceremony

A *Shintō*-style wedding is held in front of a shrine. The bride and groom drink from cups filled with sacred *saké*, then exchange their nuptial vows. This ceremony is generally attended only by direct family members of the bride and groom.

Funerals

A Buddhist-style funeral consists primarily of the *shōkō* ritual, in which each participant offers incense, and bids silent farewell to the spirit of the departed.

Compulsory education in Japan includes six years of elementary school and three years of junior high school — nine years in all. Senior high school runs for three years and college for four, meaning that if everything goes smoothly, a college graduate will enter the job market at the age of 22.

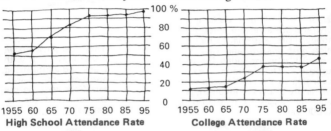

High School Attendance Rate

College Attendance Rate

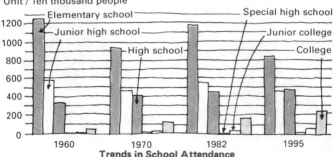

Unit / Ten thousand people

Trends in School Attendance

Japan's compulsory education attendance rate is nearly 100 percent, with 93 percent of males and 96 percent of females proceeding on to senior high, and 40 percent of males and 48 percent of females going on to four-year universities or two-year junior colleges. Clearly, Japan now ranks as one of the most educated nations in the world.

Elementary School Students

Almost all Japanese elementary school students carry a special knapsack known as a *randoseru* on their backs. Ordinary clothes (as opposed to school uniforms) are the rule, with yellow helmets worn to facilitate group commuting to school.

Junior High School Students

Public junior high school uniforms for boys normally consist of black closed collar jackets, matching black pants, a black school cap, and white canvas shoes. Some junior high schools in the countryside demand that boys keep their hair closely cropped.

Around the October 10 *Taiiku-no-hi* (Sports Day), athletic meets are held at elementary, junior and senior high schools around Japan, with all students taking part. Most of these meets feature competition between classes, with the winning class receiving trophies or other prizes.

At many junior high schools, it is common for all students to participate in sports or other club activities outside of school hours. For sports, teams often practice on holidays or early in the morning.

73

MEDICAL CARE

医療

Japan has developed an extensive medical insurance program. Since the 1958 adoption of national insurance available to the entire population, any individual may receive normal health care services at a reasonable charge. Together with this and other insurance programs, improved health care quality, higher public hygiene and other factors have helped give the Japanese one of the longest life expectancies in the world.

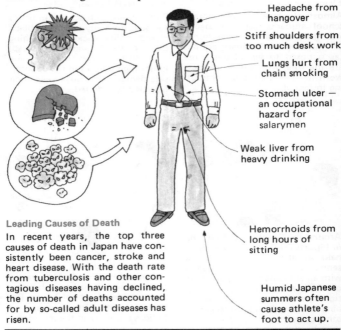

Headache from hangover

Stiff shoulders from too much desk work

Lungs hurt from chain smoking

Stomach ulcer — an occupational hazard for salarymen

Weak liver from heavy drinking

Hemorrhoids from long hours of sitting

Humid Japanese summers often cause athlete's foot to act up.

Leading Causes of Death

In recent years, the top three causes of death in Japan have consistently been cancer, stroke and heart disease. With the death rate from tuberculosis and other contagious diseases having declined, the number of deaths accounted for by so-called adult diseases has risen.

Going to the Hospital

Japanese hospitals are divided into general and specialized types. General hospitals are set up to handle most all health problems, although this often results in large numbers of patients and long waits. When the symptoms are not serious, it is often more convenient to visit specialized hospitals in the immediate neighborhood.

With the exception of many dentists, Japanese hospitals rarely require appointments. Patients may report to the hospital anytime during business hours to be examined.

The patient presents their insurance certificate at the window, gives a simple explanation of the problem, and waits their turn with the doctor.

When the examination is over, the bill is paid at the window, and medicine received. At a dentist's office, the date and time for the next appointment are decided.

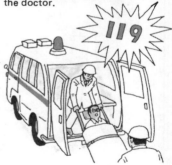

Ambulances may be summoned by telephoning 119. This is a 24-hour service, with patients taken to the nearest emergency hospital.

警察と消防

Japan enjoys remarkably fine public order compared to other countries, and it is possible to live with peace of mind even in a big city like Tokyo. Along with the national character of the Japanese people, this situation is the result of the development of a superb peace-keeping system over the years.

(Fireman)

If your residence catches on fire or you see a blaze in progress, telephone "119" to summon the fire department. This is the same number that is used to call ambulances.

(Policeman)

When experiencing or witnessing a crime, telephone "110" to summon the police.

Policeman & police box: vol. 1 p.121

Kōban (Police Box)

The *kōban* is a small police post, which can be found on street corners around the city. The officers who man these posts provide services closely tailored to the community needs. This is especially true in the countryside, where the role of policemen often goes beyond mere peace-keeping, to include lending an ear to the troubles of local people and other everyday chores.

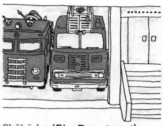

Shōbōsho (Fire Department)

Japanese fire departments house fire trucks and ambulances. They naturally stay open 24 hours, standing ready to combat fires or come to the aid of accident victims or the ill.

Possession of Firearms

Other than certain hunting use shotguns, the possession of firearms is fiercely banned.

Driving Drunk

Even if only drinking a minimal amount, driving under the influence of alcohol is a taboo in Japan.

Marijuana

The possession, use or sale of marijuana and all other narcotics is a serious breach of Japanese law.

What Not to Do in Japan

There are certain actions, which although permitted or tolerated in other nations, are strictly forbidden in Japan.

THE JAPANESE DIET

日本人の食生活

The staple food of the Japanese people is rice. Furthermore, with the country surrounded by ocean, fish are in plentiful supply, and a wide variety of marine dishes have existed since days of old. In recent years, however, the Japanese are taking a greater liking to western-style cuisine.

Japanese Restaurants

Shops specializing in *sushi, tempura* and other Japanese-style dishes hang "half curtains" *(noren)* over their entrances. When these curtains are placed outside, it is a sign that the shop is open, while pulling them inside means business hours are over.

Zashiki (Tatami Mat Seating Areas)

Besides tables and counters, many Japanese restaurants also offer *tatami* mat rooms or areas. Customers remove their shoes before entering these areas, and sit directly on the mat to dine.

See vol. 3 "Eating in Japan"

How to Hold Chopsticks

The upper chopstick is held between the index and middle fingers, and moved up and down.

The lower chopstick is held between the thumb and ring finger, and remains stationary.

Maneuvered with skill, chopsticks can even be used to pick up beans or other tiny morsels.

Japanese Table Manners

The following practices should be avoided during meals.

Clutching the chopsticks like this is considered bad manners.

Zuborabashi
Holding the chopsticks and rice bowl in the same hand.

Yosebashi
Moving a bowl forward with the chopsticks.

Tsukibashi
Skewering food with the chopsticks.

Saguribashi
Digging through a common dish of food to locate a tasty morsel.

Mayoibashi
Hovering over the table with chopsticks poised, pondering what to eat.

REPRESENTATIVE JAPANESE CUISINE

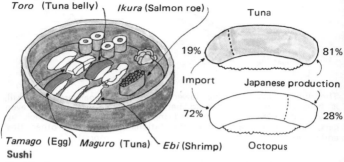

Toro (Tuna belly) *Ikura* (Salmon roe)

Tuna

19%   81%

Import   Japanese production

72%   28%

Octopus

Tamago (Egg) *Maguro* (Tuna) *Ebi* (Shrimp)

Sushi

Sushi refers to small slices or portions of fish served on pieces of vinegared rice, and ranks as one of the most popular types of Japanese cuisine.

The majority of ingredients used in *sushi* are imported.

chirashizushi

makizushi

Besides the conventional type of *nigirizushi* (fish on small rice balls), there is also *makizushi* (handrolled fish and rice), *chirashizushi* (slices of various types of fish arranged on rice in a small bowl), and more.

Shiitaké (Mushroom)

Ebi (Shrimp)

Oshinko (Pickled vegetables)
Tentsuyu (*Tempura* dip broth)

Tempura

Tempura features shrimp and other sea foods, eggplant, onions and other vegetables deep fried in a light batter known as *koromo*.

Soba (Noodles)

Soba is a slender form of noodle made from buckwheat flour, and is the most popular noodle dish in Eastern Japan.

The Japanese are fond of "slurping" their noodles in pleasantly noisy fashion.

Cold Noodles

These noodles are boiled, chilled, and then dipped in a soy-sauce flavored soup to eat.

When *aburaagé* (fried soybean curd) is placed on top of *udon* in soup, the dish becomes *kitsuné udon*.

Udon

Udon is a comparatively thick type of noodles made from wheat flour, and ranks as the most popular noodle dish in Western Japan.

Hot Noodles

Noodles are poured into a soy-sauce base soup, with shrimp *tempura*, chicken meat and other morsels placed on top.

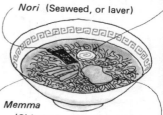

Naruto
(Steamed fish paste cake)

Nori (Seaweed, or laver)

Memma
(Chinese bamboo garnish)

Rāmen   *Chāshū* (Roast pork)

Rāmen is a Chinese dish which has been revamped for the Japanese palate. It ranks with *soba* and *udon* as one of the popular forms of Japanese noodle cuisine.

While the national sport of Japan is *sumō* wrestling, the most popular sport in the nation is clearly baseball. Also widely practiced are *jūdō*, *karaté* and other martial arts, at which the Japanese are quite skillful. *Kendō* (Japanese-style fencing) has also been carried on since the *samurai* age, and has a considerable following as a traditional martial art.

Sumō

Sumō tournaments are held six times a year, in the following cities:

- January: Tōkyō
- March: Ōsaka
- May: Tōkyō
- July: Nagoya
- September: Tōkyō
- November: Fukuoka

Each tournament lasts for 15 days, with each wrestler participating in one bout per day.

Yokozuna

Gyōji — referee

Dohyō

The ranking of the wrestlers is known as the *banzuké*. At the summit are the *yokozuna* (Grand Champions), followed by the *ōzeki* (Champions), *sekiwaké* (Junior Champions), and so forth.

Sumō matches are held in elevated circular *dohyō* rings built in the center of the arena, with two wrestlers wearing only *mawashi* (loincloth belts) going head to head. The bout is decided when one wrestler throws his opponent down or out of the ring.

O-zumō: vol.1 p.122/vol.16 p.22
Watching Sumō or baseball: vol.2 p.92/vol.16 p.64/vol.17 p.137

Baseball

Japanese professional baseball consists of two six-team leagues, known as the Central and Pacific Leagues.

Central League Teams

Yomiuri Giants   (Tōkyō)
Yakult Swallows   (Tōkyō)
Yokohama Bay Stars   (Yokohama)
Chūnichi Dragons   (Nagoya)
Hanshin Tigers   (Ōsaka)
Hiroshima Carp   (Hiroshima)

Pacific League Teams

Nippon Ham Fighters (Tōkyō)
Seibu Lions   (Tokorozawa)
Lotte Marines   (Chiba)
Orix Blue Wave   (Nishinomiya)
Daiei Hawks   (Fukuoka)
Kintetsu Buffaloes   (Ōsaka)

The outfield cheering sections in Japanese baseball are well-organized, with the members decked out in the proper colors of uniforms, and trumpets and drums used to cheer on the teams to victory.

In addition to the pros, the high-school baseball national tournaments held twice annually (in the spring and summer) also attract widespread media and fan attention.

TRADITIONAL AMUSEMENTS

伝統的な娯楽

By far the most famous form of indigenous Japanese entertainment is the *kabuki* theater. Other amusements cultivated through Japan's long history and tradition include *Noh* plays, *Bunraku* (puppet theater), *Rakugo* (comic storytelling) and more.

Nimaimé (A handsome male actor)

Oyama (Or Onnagata)
Kabuki is performed exclusively by male actors, with men also handling the roles of women. Actors specializing in female roles (and the costumes and make-up which accompany them) are known as *Oyama*.

Aragoto (A style of acting which expresses anger)

Kabuki

The *kabuki* stage is equipped with a wide range of tricks and contraptions, geared to thrill and amaze the audience.

Noh

Noh plays are performed by the *shité* (main protagonist) and *waki* (supporting actor). The slow and beautiful movements of the actors and quiet and monotonous nature of the background music serve to lure the audience into the realm of dreams.

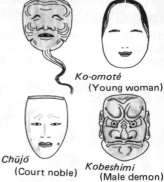

Okina (Old man)

Ko-omoté (Young woman)

Chūjō (Court noble)

Kobeshimi (Male demon)

Noh actors cover their faces with special role masks.

The *bunraku* dialogue consists of verbal narratives known as *jōruri.*

Bunraku (Puppet Theater)

Together with *kabuki, bunraku* is a popular entertainment handed down from the *Edo* period. The skillful manipulation of elaborate puppets by veteran puppeteers brings superb drama and tension to the stories being told.

The *Rakugo* comedian uses a *sensu* (folding fan), *tenugui* (hand-towel) and other props to create amusing expressions.

Chopsticks and dish

Rakugo (Comic Storytelling)

Rakugo, a comic narrative style originating in the *Edo* period, which now enjoys a wide popular following.

MODERN-DAY RECREATION

現代的な娯楽

How do the modern-day Japanese get their kicks? In this section, we introduce several popular methods of recreation considered to be particurly "Japanese" in nature.

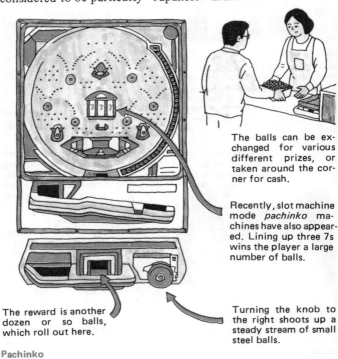

The balls can be exchanged for various different prizes, or taken around the corner for cash.

Recently, slot machine mode *pachinko* machines have also appeared. Lining up three 7s wins the player a large number of balls.

The reward is another dozen or so balls, which roll out here.

Turning the knob to the right shoots up a steady stream of small steel balls.

Pachinko

A game indigenous to Japan, *pachinko* is one of the most popular recreations enjoyed by businessmen and other Japanese.

Mahjong
This board game is another popular amusement in Japan. In the case of businessmen, however, it is often played with important clients, making the game an extension of their work duties.

Horseracing
Horseracing ranks with *pachinko* and *mahjong* as a traditional Japanese recreation. Together with bicycle and motor boat racing, horseracing is one of the few legal means to gamble in Japan.

Golf
Golf is very popular among businessmen in Japan. Many, however, find themselves forced to learn the sport in order to help entertain clients.

Computer Game Software
Most households with children today own Computer game software. Even so, parents have been known to get more involved in this electronic mania than their children.

RELIGION

宗教

While Japan's native religion is *Shintō*, the teachings of the Buddha were carried to the nation from the sixth century, and there have been many historical periods in which Buddhism was actually considered the official national faith. Missionaries began to spread Christianity from the 16th century, and the mix of these three major religions continues to the current day.

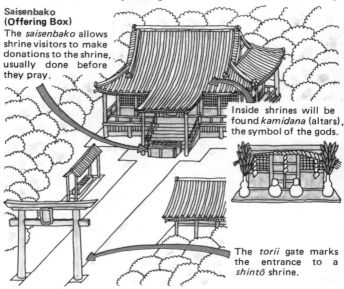

Saisenbako (Offering Box)
The *saisenbako* allows shrine visitors to make donations to the shrine, usually done before they pray.

Inside shrines will be found *kamidana* (altars), the symbol of the gods.

The *torii* gate marks the entrance to a *shintō* shrine.

Jinja (Shrines)
Shrines are locations for the worship of the gods of *Shintō*. Originally a form of animism, *Shintō* holds that mountains, trees, the skies and all other things in the natural world are endowed with their own gods.

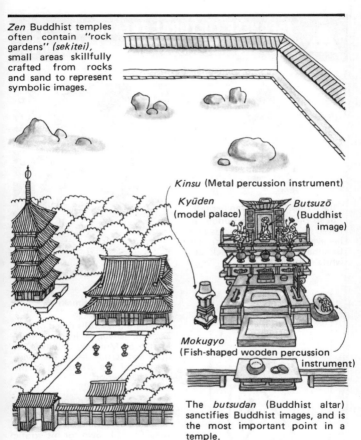

Zen Buddhist temples often contain "rock gardens" *(sekitei)*, small areas skillfully crafted from rocks and sand to represent symbolic images.

Kinsu (Metal percussion instrument)

Kyūden (model palace)

Butsuzō (Buddhist image)

Mokugyo (Fish-shaped wooden percussion instrument)

The *butsudan* (Buddhist altar) sanctifies Buddhist images, and is the most important point in a temple.

Jiin (Temples)

Temples are locations for the worship of the Buddha. There are various schools of Buddhism, with the specific Buddha worshipped varying from sect to sect.

Paintings

Fugen Bosatsuzō (Heian period)
Fugen Bosatsu is the Buddha believed to be the guardian saint of believers of the Lotus Sutra. This Buddha rides on the back of a white elephant.

Genji Monogatari Emaki
(Heian period)

These are the scrolls based on *The Tales of Genji,* a lengthy novel written by Murasaki Shikibu. The story and scrolls depict the lavish lifestyle of the aristocrats in the late Heian period.

Kanzanzu (Northern and Southern Court period)

Kanzan was a Buddhist priest of Tang China known for his erratic behavior. The bold style and precise design make this one of the true masterpieces of Japanese Indian ink painting.

Butsuzō (Buddhist Images)

Miroku Bosatsu Hankazō
(Asuka period, 7th century)

The principal image of the Maitreya Bodhisattva at Kōryū-ji Temple in Kyoto. This work dates from the early days of Buddhist influence in Japan, and is famous for the subject's penetrating beauty and mystical smile. There is a story of a tourist who, overcome with her beauty, leaped to hug the lady, and broke his little finger.

Kongō Rikishi Ritsuzō
(Kamakura period, 13th century)

The "Deva King" — another sculpture masterpiece from the Kamakura era. The angry expression, sharply arched eyebrows and swelling muscles reflect the dominating style of the sculpture of this age. Currently stored in Tōdai-ji Temple in Nara.

Raijin
(Kamakura period, 13th century)

The fierce gods of thunder. *Raijin* beats the drum on his back to conjure up thunder.

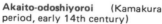

Shishū Shaka Nyorai Seppōzu
(Nara period)

An embroidery based on the theme of the preaching Buddha, using red, brown, scarlet, green, blue and other colored thread. The overwhelming three-dimensional sense of this expression strongly reflects the Tang China influence.

Akaito-odoshiyoroi (Kamakura period, early 14th century)

A highly ceremonial version of *samurai* armor, characterized by red thread embroidery and lavish metal carvings.

Tamamushi-no-zushi
(Asuka period)

A container used to house Buddhist images and scriptures, now stored in Hōryū-ji Temple in Nara. An exquisite blend of the building, woodworking, metalworking, lacquering, painting and other techniques of the Asuka era.

Kiyomizu Temple Hondō
(Edo period, 1633)

The main pavilion of Kiyomizu Temple, located in Higashiyama in Kyōto. It features a unique style, in which the building faces out over a high precipice, with the floor supported by long pillars. It ranks as a masterpiece of Japanese-style architecture of the early Edo period.

Hōryū-ji Temple Five-Storied Pagoda (Asuka period, late 7th to early 8th century)

One of the oldest wooden structures in the world, still retaining its superb beauty a thousand years after being erected. Together with the Golden Pavilion of Hōryū-ji, this pagoda reflects the superb quality of traditional Japanese wooden architecture.

Byōdō-in Temple Phoenix Pavilion
(Heian period, 1053)

Constructed by Fujiwara Michinaga, the most powerful man of the Heian age, the beauty of this pavilion was widely believed to be a reproduction of the "Pure Land" (Buddhist Paradise) on earth.

CASTLES

城

The Japanese castle is a distinctive architectural form developed in the 16 - 17th century, during the nation's Age of Warring States. Centered around a high tower known as the *tenshukaku*, these castles were surrounded by moats *(hori)* to keep out potential invaders.

Most castle towers are mounted with decorative sculptures of the *shachihoko* fish. According to Chinese legend, this fish spouts out water in case of fire, with the sculpture thus expressing the importance of fire prevention.

Stones are dropped to repel the invading *ninja*.

Castles were rigged with a wide range of mechanisms to keep out hostile forces.

TRANSPORTATION AND COMMUNICATIONS

交通と通信

OVERVIEW

Transportation in Japan has grown extremely advanced, with trains, buses and other publics systems offering efficient and convenient travel to almost any part of the country. The punctuality of Japanese train schedules has no pier anywhere in the world, and during commuting hours in Tōkyō and other big cities trains often leave stations at three-minute intervals.

Japan produces more automobiles than any nation in the world, and its motorization is rapidly reaching a scale comparable with that of America. In Tōkyō and other major urban centers, however, heavy congestion, narrow roads and one-way streets are the rule, making it difficult for unaccustomed drivers to get around.

The country is also well equipped with telephones, postal services, and other communications networks. Public phones can be found on most street corners, and very few ever break down. Mail delivery, meanwhile, is famous for its accuracy, with very few lost or wandering letters.

Japan has six major television stations, which present a rich range of programming from early in the morning until late at night. Over 95 percent of households subscribe to a newspaper, with some major nationwide dailies boasting circulation of over eight million. One negative effect of this mass media development, however, is a steady trend toward cultural homogeneity, and many of Japan's distinctive regional customs and traditions are beginning to fade.

SHINKANSEN

新幹線

The *Shinkansen* "bullet train" is Japan's most renowned express train, and travels at the maximum speed of 270 km/hr. The first leg of this line was completed between Tōkyō and Ōsaka in 1964, the year of the Tōkyō Olympics, followed by the *Sanyō*, *Tōhoku* and *Jōetsu* branches in subsequent years.

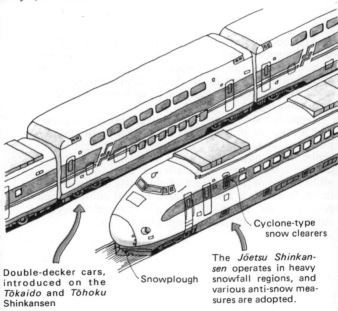

Cyclone-type snow clearers

The *Jōetsu Shinkansen* operates in heavy snowfall regions, and various anti-snow measures are adopted.

Double-decker cars, introduced on the *Tōkaido* and *Tōhoku* Shinkansen

Snowplough

16-car trains on the *Tōkaidō* Shinkansen accommodate 1,277 passengers. There are also special seats available for disabled passengers.

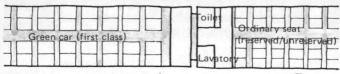

Shinkansen cars contain rows of two and three seats. Private compartments have also been introduced on some cars.

Many items are sold en route, including box lunches *(obentō)*, drinks, regional delicacy souvenirs, and more.

Public telephones are provided, and offer service to the major cities along the route. Calls may also be placed to specific *Shinkansen* trains, to have passengers paged.

Linear motor car

The JR group is currently advancing development of a linear motor car, destined to be the next-generation super-speed train after the *Shinkansen*.

HSST

A new transportation mode being developed by Japan Air Lines, scheduled to link airports to the cities. Development began in 1974, with working models displayed at the world expositions in Tsukuba, Japan in 1985, and Vancouver, British Columbia (Canada) in 1986.

RAILWAY AND ROADMAP

幹線と高速道路マップ

1 Tōkaidō Shinkansen (Bullet Train)
2 San'yō Shinkansen (Bullet Train)
3 Tōhoku Shinkansen (Bullet Train)
4 Yamagata Shinkansen (Bullet Train)
5 Akita Shinkansen (Bullet Train)
6 Jōetsu Shinkansen (Bullet Train)
7 Nagano Shinkansen (Bullet Train)
8 Nemuro Trunk Line
9 Muroran Trunk Line
10 Hakodaté Trunk Line
11 Seikan Tunnel
12 Tōhoku Trunk Line
13 Ohu Trunk Line

14 Uetsu Trunk Line
15 Jōban Line
16 Chūō Trunk Line
17 Tōkaidō Trunk Line
18 Shinétsu Trunk Line
19 Hokuriku Trunk Line
20 San'yō Trunk Line
21 San'in Trunk Line
22 Seto Ōhashi Bridges
23 Yosan Line
24 Dosan Line
25 Nippō Trunk Line
26 Kagoshima Trunk Line

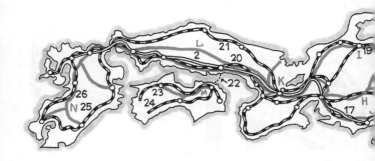

A Dōoh Motorway
B Tōhoku Jūkan Motorway
C Ban'etsu Motorway
D Jōban Motorway
E Higashi Kantō Motorway
F Kan'etsu Motorway
G Jōshin'etsu Motorway
H Chūō Motorway
I Hokuriku Motorway
J Tōmei Expressway
K Meishin Expressway
L Chūgoku Jyūkan Motorway
M Shikoku Jyūkan Motorway
N Kyūshū Jyūkan Motorway

The railroad is the form of transportation most often used by overseas travelers visiting Japan. Skillful use of these systems will expand the sphere of one's mobility, and provide a more enjoyable, efficient and economical trip.

JR Ticket Vending Machines

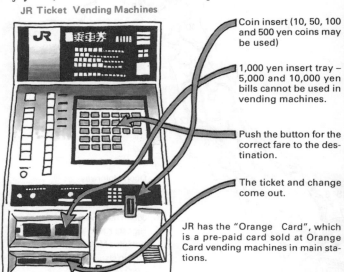

Coin insert (10, 50, 100 and 500 yen coins may be used)

1,000 yen insert tray – 5,000 and 10,000 yen bills cannot be used in vending machines.

Push the button for the correct fare to the destination.

The ticket and change come out.

JR has the "Orange Card", which is a pre-paid card sold at Orange Card vending machines in main stations.

Riding City Trains

Japanese railways may be broadly divided into the city trains which serve urban areas, and the long-distance trains which link up different cities and regions. City trains may be classified into Japan Railway (JR), the private railways, and the subways, although all three types are utilized in basically the same way.

Getting on the train

When arriving at a station, first check the fare schedule posted over the vending machine to find the cost to your destination. Some stations in Tōkyō and other large stations provide signs in Roman letters.

After purchasing a ticket, have it checked by the automatic fare collection gates, and walk to the platform. This ticket is proof of where you boarded, so hold onto it until leaving the gate at your destination station.

Larger stations are divided into several different platforms. Signs will guide you to the platform entrance, where you should confirm the platform from which your train is leaving.

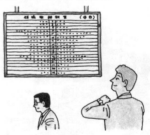

The platforms contain train schedule boards, enabling passengers to check on the departure time of their trains. Japanese trains almost always leave on schedule. Keep in mind that in big cities, these schedule boards are divided into weekday and holiday (Sundays and national holidays) panels.

Getting off the train

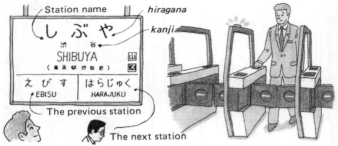

Station name — *hiragana*
— *kanji*

しぶや
渋谷
SHIBUYA
（東京都渋谷区）

えびす | はらじゅく
EBISU | HARAJUKU

The previous station

The next station

The platforms contain large signs bearing the name of the station. The name will appear in both Japanese characters and Roman letters, making it easy to check on which station the train has arrived at.

Insert your ticket to the automatic fare collection gates, and exit. Tickets which don't cover the required fare may be adjusted right there, although it is more efficient to use the nearby fare adjustment machine.

Entrance signs contain the names of buildings and other major landmarks in the immediate vicinity.

ハチ公口 北口 ↑
新玉川線 地下鉄（eorus）

At the fare adjustment machine, insert your ticket, pay the balance due, and receive a special ticket. Insert this ticket to the ticket collector back at the wicket, and exit.

Big stations will have several different exits, and it is a good idea to check on which exit is most convenient to your particular destination.

104

Taking the train: vol.2 p.24

Timetable books may be purchased which list all JR and other railway routes, departure and arrival times, fares and other information. These inexpensive volumes are a must for travel buffs, and a handy tool for anyone taking a trip.

Shinkansen (Bullet Train) and other long-distance train tickets may be purchased at the proper station counter. Reserved seats go on sale exactly one month before departure, and are handled at the *Midori-no-Madoguchi* (counter areas distinguished by green sign boards).

Kuroshio ("Black Current")

Hokkaidō Japan Railway Company

East Japan Railway Company
Central Japan Railway Company
West Japan Railway Company

Odoriko ("Dancing Girl")

Shikoku Japan Railway Company

Kyūshū Japan Railway Company

Hayabusa ("Falcon")

The long-distance trains are christened with various different colorful names.

Riding long-distance trains

The vast majority of long-distance trains are operated by the JR group. Although JR is divided up into six separate companies, the fare schedule is identical for all of them, and there is no need to purchase different tickets for different JR firms.

BUSES

バス

Buses are the most important means of public transportation in regions where the railways have not been widely developed. Also operated are highway buses for long-distance travelers, and regularly scheduled sightseeing buses for tourists.

Tōkyō city buses

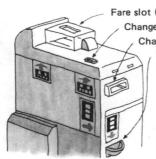

Fare ticket slot

Fare slot (When no change is necessary)

Change in coin

Change in note

When change is required, place the coins in here.

The bus fare in the 23 wards of Tōkyō is 200 yen for adults and 100 yen for children.

The fare is dropped into the coin box beside the driver. All kinds of coin and 1000 yen note are acceptable. No change can be given for 5000 yen and 10000 yen note.

Riding City Buses

On buses operating in Tōkyō and other big cities, there is a set fare for riding within specified areas. Passengers board at the front of the bus, where they pay the fare. When the bus comes to their stop, they exit at the rear door.

Using the municipal buses: vol.2 p.28

The display at the front of the bus shows the current fare by ticket number.

The fare and ticket are placed in the fare box.

Buses for which the fare varies by the distance ridden are boarded from the rear, where a numbered ticket is taken. The fare is paid when getting off, and placed in the box next to the driver.

The ticket number indicates where the passenger boarded.

Push the buzzer on the window side of the seat just before the bus approaches your stop. Each stop is announced in Japanese, but if you don't understand the language well you may want to alert the driver of where you want to get off when you board.

Hato Bus
Hato Buses are privately operated sightseeing buses in the Tōkyō area. The company also operates many double-decker buses.

Japan has a high volume of taxis compared to the U.S. and Europe, making it relatively easy to hail a cab. Cabby manners are good and the fares are clearly posted, making this a fairly reliable means of getting around.

A red sign in the front window of a cab indicates that the vehicle is for hire.

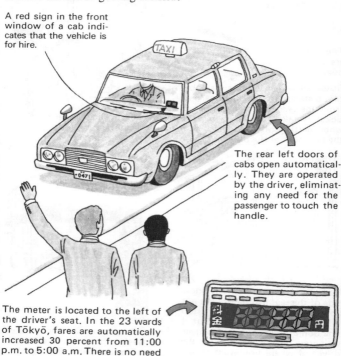

The rear left doors of cabs open automatically. They are operated by the driver, eliminating any need for the passenger to touch the handle.

The meter is located to the left of the driver's seat. In the 23 wards of Tōkyō, fares are automatically increased 30 percent from 11:00 p.m. to 5:00 a.m. There is no need to tip cab drivers in Japan.

Taking a taxi: vol.2 p.30

DRIVING

車

The rent-a-car industry is widely developed in Japan, and most anyone with a driver's license can rent a car without problem. However, the large number of vehicles, traffic congestion, and narrow roads make it somewhat difficult for overseas travelers to truly savor the pleasure of motoring in Japan.

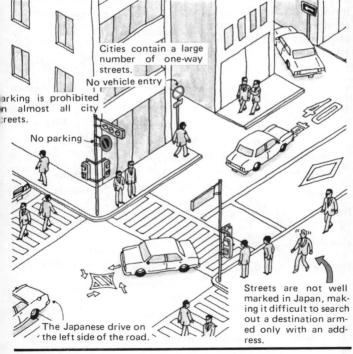

Cities contain a large number of one-way streets.

No vehicle entry

Parking is prohibited in almost all city streets.

No parking

Streets are not well marked in Japan, making it difficult to search out a destination armed only with an address.

The Japanese drive on the left side of the road.

AIRPLANES

飛行機

The domestic airways in Japan are largely covered by three companies – Japan Airlines (JAL), All Nippon Airways (ANA) and Japan Air System (JAS). As well, in 1998 Skymark Airlines began regular low-cost service between Tokyo and Fukuoka. While Air Do began it between Tokyo and Hakodaté. Tickets may be purchased at Japan Travel Bureau (JTB) offices or other travel agents. Telephone reservations may also be made at air lines reservation service centers.

Major airports and major routes from Tokyo

BOATS

船

Japan is an archipelago made up of several thousand islands. The shipping industry has been well developed from days of old, with a vast number of sea routes used to link up the nation's ports. However, passenger travel is now largely dominated by trains and planes, with few people choosing to take extended trips by water.

Nippon-Maru
A representative Japanese ocean-going passenger liner.

Phoenix Express
The ferry connecting Kawasaki and Hyūga, in Miyazaki prefecture.

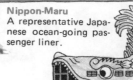

Kinko (Nagoya)

Many sightseeing boats operate of lakes and bays around Japan.

Super City
The sightseeing boat on the Sumida river in Tokyo. The roof of some boats are opened as the deck.

Victoria (Ashinoko Lake)

There are three major travel seasons in Japan — the so-called "Golden Week" from late April through early May, *Bon* in mid-August, and the New Year's holiday at the turn of the year. All modes of transportation become extremely congested during these seasons.

Popular sightseeing spots in Japan

Kyōto   Karuizawa   Izu

Shūgaku Ryokō (School Excursions)

In the spring and fall, groups of junior and senior high school students can often be seen traveling by train or bus. Many stop off at *Kyōto* or *Nara,* where they tour temples and other cultural sites, or at *Hiroshima,* where they ponder the remains of the world's first nuclear attack, and cultivate a greater appreciation of the value of peace. Junior high school students from the outlying regions can frequently be seen exploring the chic *Harajuku* district of Tōkyō.

College students

Down to the beaches in the summer to surf, up to the mountains in winter to ski, with tennis training camps picking up the slack in the spring and fall. The senior year summer vacation is often used as an opportunity to travel abroad, funded by the earnings saved from part-time jobs worked up to that point.

Young OL (office ladies)

Young OL (office ladies) take their paid vacation all at once, using salary bonuses to travel to Hawaii, Guam or other popular locations.

A favorite among Japanese children is Tōkyō Disneyland.

Family Trips

All popular tourist spots are packed during peak travel seasons, and family outings can often generate more exhaustion than enjoyment.

Onsen (Hot springs)

A land of many volcanoes, Japan is noted for its wealth of hot spring resorts. Rustic country spas are no longer frequented only by the elderly, with young women also flocking to these natural baths in recent years.

NEWSPAPERS
新聞

Japanese newspapers are delivered both in the morning and evening, a system rare throughout the world. The subscription rate is extremely high, and newspapers serve as one of the country's most important news media.

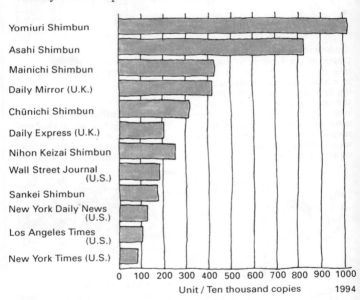

Yomiuri Shimbun	
Asahi Shimbun	
Mainichi Shimbun	
Daily Mirror (U.K.)	
Chūnichi Shimbun	
Daily Express (U.K.)	
Nihon Keizai Shimbun	
Wall Street Journal (U.S.)	
Sankei Shimbun	
New York Daily News (U.S.)	
Los Angeles Times (U.S.)	
New York Times (U.S.)	

0 100 200 300 400 500 600 700 800 900 1000
Unit / Ten thousand copies   1994

Major world newspapers and circulation volume (morning editions)

Newspapers may be divided into nationwide papers, which maintain sales networks throughout the country, and regional papers, which concentrate on service in their particular districts. The largest nationwide paper currently boasts circulation of over 10 million copies.

Many households subscribe to a combination of nationwide, regional, economic, sports, and other types of newspapers, with an average subscription rate of 1.3 papers.

Sports and evening newspapers are available at almost all station concession stands.

Sports Newspapers

Sports newspapers focus on articles about baseball, the most popular sport in Japan, and also cover the entertainment business, horseracing and other gambling, fishing, and other types of recreation. On the strength of their upbeat content, these papers are widely read by the businessmen on morning commuter trains.

Evening papers

Tabloid style evening newspapers, which specialize in sensationalized reports of social incidents, political scandals, and other hot news, are widely read by businessmen on the trains going home.

Home delivery of newspapers is handled by young part-timers who make their rounds on bicycles. Many of these workers receive lodging at newspaper sales outlets, carrying on their delivery work while commuting to college or pursuing other goals.

Newspaper circulation has a sharp impact on advertising sales, and the marketing competition between the larger papers is fierce indeed. Salesmen in big cities commonly use towels, baseball tickets or other presents to entice potential customers.

PUBLICATIONS

出版

The Japanese love to read, and over five billion books and weekly and monthly magazines are printed annually.

Unit/Billion copies

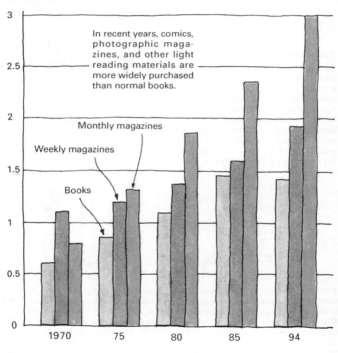

In recent years, comics, photographic magazines, and other light reading materials are more widely purchased than normal books.

Monthly magazines

Weekly magazines

Books

1970   75   80   85   94

Copies published

Top-selling publications

Juvenile comics

Juvenile comic books, originally created with elementary school readers in mind, enjoy explosive popularity among college students and businessmen as well. The stories feature simple plots, dealing with love, justice, friendship and other pertinent themes.

Girl's comics

These comics target teenage girls, with their heroines depicted with sparkling, oversized eyes. Also published recently, however, are many works of fantasy with high artistic sense.

Weekly photo magazines

Weekly magazines focusing on photographs geared to stir up gossip about famous personalities and other controversy, currently sell at a rate of around three million copies weekly.

Women's fashion magazines

The most popular magazines among young women in their teens and 20s are photographic fashion mags. Besides pure fashion, they offer news about the latest trends in cuisine, travel, sports and other recreation and entertainment.

TELEVISION

テレビ

There has been a rapid increase in television ownership in Japan since the 1960s, and life without the "boob tube" is truly a thing of the past.

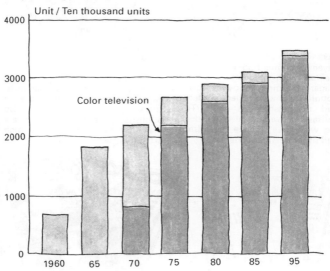

Unit / Ten thousand units

Color television

1960 65 70 75 80 85 95

Number of television "subscribers"

This refers to the number of households which pay the socalled "subscription fee" for NHK (the Japan Broadcasting Corporation). As such, the number of TV sets actually in use is much higher.

In addition to the nationally managed NHK (which offers both a general and education channel), 7500 private sector broadcasting stations are also operated in Japan. Acting as the "key stations" in the production of their programming are TBS, NTV, Television Asahi, Fuji Television, and Television Tōkyō.

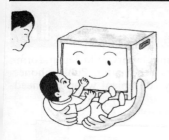

Terebikko ("TV Generation")

With the increase in the number of television sets, many mothers allow the TV to look after and entertain their children. Members of the generation raised in front of the television are known as *terebikko* (literally, "TV kids").

Recent years have seen the rise of video, Computer games, and other new styles of entertainment using the TV screen. Cable television and satellite broadcasts are also getting off the ground, with television continuing to increase its importance to the Japanese as a mass media.

TV heroes

Mito Kōmon

A *samurai* period piece set in the Edo period, in which an old man and several loyal retainers travel around Japan, encountering human drama and punishing the bad guys.

Sazaé-san

Broadcast for over three decades, this weekly cartoon show treats various lifestyle themes in the household of an average Japanese family. Naturally, the characters do not age.

Doraemon

An ingenious robot cat from the future. Producing a delightful range of tools and other magical wonders from his front pouch, *Doraemon* makes the dreams of children come true.

There are some 61 million telephones in service in Japan, forming a network linking every corner of the nation. Public phones rarely break down, making it very convenient when you need to place a call from the outside.

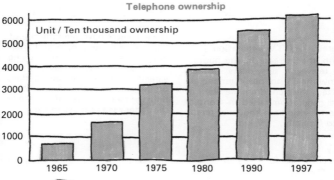

Telephone ownership

Unit / Ten thousand ownership

For emergency calls, push this button without inserting any money, and you will be directly connected to the police or fire department. To call the police dial 110, and for the fire department or an ambulance, call 119.

Handy telephone numbers to remember:

English language information for travelers

Tōkyō:	03-3502-1461
Kyōto:	075-371-5649
International call operator(KDD):	0051

Types of public phones

Most pay phones in Japan are green or gray. With them you can use telephone cards, and many let you insert 10 and 100 yen coins.

Coin slots

Public phones accept 10 and 100 yen coins. The charge for calls within the same area code is 10 yen per minute.
No charge is given for 100 yen coins, even if the call doesn't require the full amount.

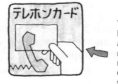

Telephone cards may be purchased in 500 and 1,000 yen denominations. From vending machines or at stores displaying this special sign.

Gray phone　　　　Green phone

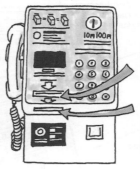

Insert the telephone card here.

When you hang up, the card is returned here.

Data jack

Both telephone cards and coins (100 and 10 yen) can be used. A buzzer will sound just before the call is cut off. This is a signal to add another 10 or 100 yen or another telephone card. You can call overseas from these types of pay phones, using 100-yen coins or a telephone card. Gray pay phones use modern digital technology, so you can connect your laptop, then send and receive electronic data.

MAIL

郵便

Japan has developed a superb postal service system. There are very few cases of late or lost mail, and no strikes by postal employees. Letters addressed in Roman letters are also delivered without problem, a major convenience for foreign residents who do not read or write Japanese.

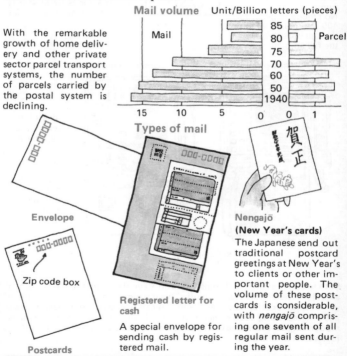

Mail volume   Unit/Billion letters (pieces)

With the remarkable growth of home delivery and other private sector parcel transport systems, the number of parcels carried by the postal system is declining.

Mail — Parcel

85 80 75 70 60 50 1940

15 10 5 0 0 1

Types of mail

Envelope

Zip code box

Postcards

Registered letter for cash

A special envelope for sending cash by registered mail.

**Nengajō
(New Year's cards)**

The Japanese send out traditional postcard greetings at New Year's to clients or other important people. The volume of these postcards is considerable, with *nengajō* comprising one seventh of all regular mail sent during the year.

賀正

122

How to send mail

Stamps may be purchased at post offices, or any store displaying this sign. Domestic rates are 50 yen for postcards and 80 yen for standard letters.

Drop boxes have two-slots—The left-hand one is for ordinary letters and postcards, while the right-hand one is for letters to overseas addresses and express delivery letters.

To send parcels, go directly to the post office. The PO is also involved in financial, life and nonlife insurance, and other business undertakings.

Rice shops and other small stores displaying the following types of signs will accept parcels for shipment through private sector home delivery systems.

Sending mail: vol.2 p.40

Development is being advanced on new communication systems which use satellites, optical cables, computer networks and other technology. This trend is bringing major changes in the lifestyles of the Japanese.

Home Shopping
The use of cable television or facsimile machines for direct purchase of goods on a mail order basis.

Home Banking
Online link-ups may be established between the bank and home, with computers used to monitor savings accounts, balance household accounts, and perform other tasks.

Computer Learning Systems
Networks linking computers to libraries and schools provide excellent learning opportunities.

Disaster Prevention
In some modern buildings, telephones can be used to control gas, water, air conditioning and other systems from outside the home.

INDUSTRY

産業

OVERVIEW

The economic development of postwar Japan is indeed the very history of the nation's industrialization. This period was characterized by a major shift in the focus of labor from primary to secondary industries, as plants were constructed on farming land, and fishing ports transformed into massive petrochemical complex.

The 10-year period centered on the 1964 Tōkyō Olympics was the climax of this accelerated economic growth, with steel, shipbuilding, heavy electric machinery and other heavy industries supporting the nation's rapid rise to prosperity.

On the other hand, this trend dealt major blows to traditional farming, forestry and fishing, with rice farming, the very fiber of Japanese history, finding itself unable to survive without large-scale economic aid from the government. It was also during this time that invironmental pollution came to be targeted as a major social problem, such as the "Minamata Disease" caused by the dumping of large amounts of organic mercury wasted into the sea.

In the 1970s, Japan's industrial structure again underwent major changes as a result of the two oil crises. As wage levels climbed, the international competitiveness of secondary industries, and especially the heavier sectors, weakened, with a steady shift to service. In 1975, workers employed in service industries came to constitute over 50 percent of the labor force, as Japan was steadily becoming a developed nation along the lines of America and Europe.

This trend has continued in the 1980s, with the surge in the strength of the Japanese yen dealing a crushing blow to steel, shipbuilding and other sectors. Banking, securities, insurance and other industries have enjoyed massive capital buildups as a result, with a tendency to strive for profits from investment in real estate and stocks, rather than through the manufacturing of products. There are some economists who read this move as a shift from the service sector to information industries using computers and other high technology, although there is certainly no guarantee that this trend will generate greater national prosperity in the long run.

UNDERGROUND RESOURCES
地下資源

Literally a "mineral museum," Japan is blessed with a rich range of underground resources. Unfortunately, the volume of the actual deposits is quite limited, forcing the country to rely on imports for the vast majority of its oil, steel, and other industrial materials.

Percentage of major underground resources imported

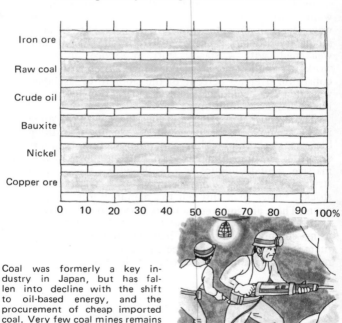

Iron ore
Raw coal
Crude oil
Bauxite
Nickel
Copper ore

0 10 20 30 40 50 60 70 80 90 100%

Coal was formerly a key industry in Japan, but has fallen into decline with the shift to oil-based energy, and the procurement of cheap imported coal. Very few coal mines remains in operation in Japan today.

WATER RESOURCES
水資源

To an agricultural people like the Japanese, water has always been a vital resource due to its use in rice farming. Although Japan is a land of comparatively heavy rainfall, its rivers are short in length, and the rain water flows quickly down to the sea. As a result, the Japanese have developed various means for effective storage and use of water over the centuries.

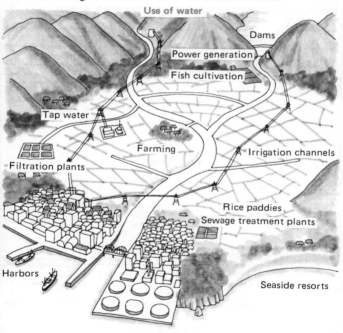

Use of water

Dams

Power generation

Fish cultivation

Tap water

Farming

Irrigation channels

Filtration plants

Rice paddies

Sewage treatment plants

Harbors

Seaside resorts

LAND USE
国土利用

Japan is a country with a large population and little land — 70 percent of which is mountainous. As a result, land is an extremely precious quantity to the Japanese. In recent years there have been rapid moves to reclaim coastal areas, excavate mountains to create housing sites, and other developments. However, this trend has not been without problems, such as environmental destruction and other negative aspects.

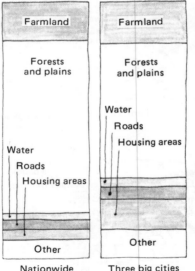

How land is used

130

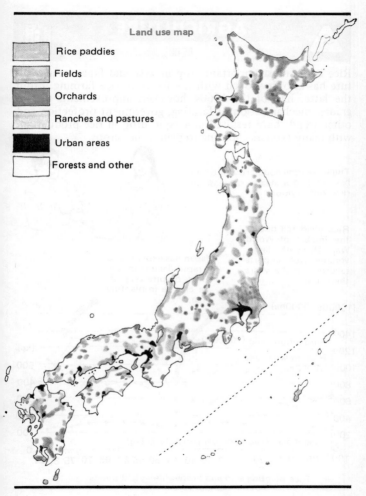

Land use map

Rice paddies
Fields
Orchards
Ranches and pastures
Urban areas
Forests and other

Rice is the most important crop in Asia, and Japanese agriculture has also developed with the focus on rice farming. From the latter half of the 1960s, however, improvements in rice grades, mechanization of farming, government protection and other trends have resulted in a rapid drop in rice production, with many farmers choosing to plant other crops.

The increasing popularity of bread has sparked a steady decrease in rice consumption.

Rice yield fell due to the impact of World War II, with large-volume rice imports recorded in the years thereafter.

Japan has experienced a rapid decline in rice yield, despite very little change in planting area.

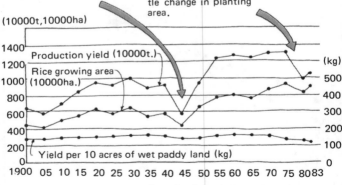

(10000t,10000ha)

- Production yield (10000t.)
- Rice growing area (10000ha.)
- Yield per 10 acres of wet paddy land (kg)

(kg)

1900 05 10 15 20 25 30 35 40 45 50 55 60 65 70 75 80 83

Rice planting area and production yield trends

How rice is grown

Cultivators are used to till the earth.

Tractors prepare the paddies.

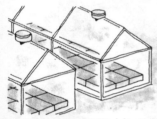

Seedlings are cultivated in greenhouses.

The seedlings are planted in the paddies.

Herbicides are spread.

Binders harvest the rice.

Tractors

Tractors developed for agricultural use are now an indispensable part of rice farming, and indeed symbolize mechanized farming in Japan.

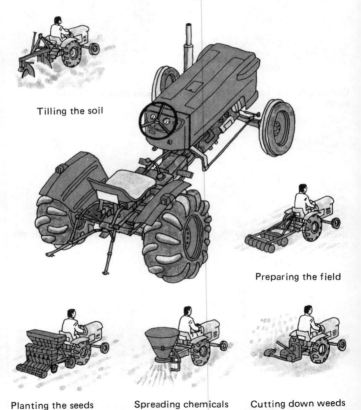

Tilling the soil

Preparing the field

Planting the seeds

Spreading chemicals

Cutting down weeds

Vegetables

Because vegetable crops are heavily influenced by the weather, there has been a sharp increase in the use of vinyl plastic or glass greenhouses to grow vegetables since the 1960s.

Fruits

Tangerines, apples, pears, *kaki* (Japanese persimmons), grapes, and other types of fruit are grown in Japan. Consumption has increased together with the improvements in living standards, while imports of grapefruits, lemons, pineapples and other fruits also on the rise.

Stockbreeding

With a diet consisting mainly of fish, Japanese stockbreeding was traditionally limited to raising cows and horses for use in farming and other work, or a handful of pigs or chickens in the backyard. With the rich diversification in the Japanese diet, however, the demand for pork and chicken has soared, leading to dynamic growth in the domestic stockbreeding industry.

Dairy Farming

Before World War II, the Japanese raised very few cows for the purpose of milk or other dairy products. The Westernization in the postwar years, however, has seen much greater milk consumption, with large-scale dairy farms now operated in Hokkaidō and other regions.

FORESTRY

林業

There are approximately 25 million hectares of forest area in Japan. Some 60 percent of this area is natural forest with large amounts of broad-leaf trees, while the remaining 40 percent is planted forest land — the focus on coniferous trees. About 50 percent of Japan's lumber comes from domestic forests, with the other half consisting of cheaper foreign wood. With today's decreasing demand for lumber, the Japanese forestry industry now finds itself at a major crossroads.

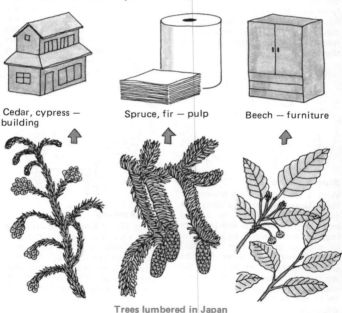

Cedar, cypress — building

Spruce, fir — pulp

Beech — furniture

Trees lumbered in Japan

Traditional Japanese wooden architecture

This type of building is slowly vanishing from Japan's cities.

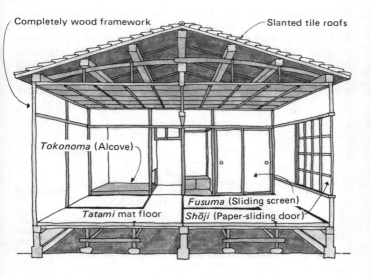

Completely wood framework

Slanted tile roofs

Tokonoma (Alcove)

Tatami mat floor

Fusuma (Sliding screen)

Shōji (Paper-sliding door)

Immediately after World War II, cedar and cypress forests were planted in mountainous areas around Japan, targeting future use in building. The shrinking demand for these materials is presenting major problems for the nation's forestry industry.

FISHERIES

漁業

Surrounded by the sea, Japan is one of world's most famous fishing nations. While Japan's traditional coastal fishing industry is being eroded by excessive catches and water pollution, major progress has been made in deep-sea fishing using large-scale boats. In more recent years, however, restrictions on fishing grounds and volume have cut into the deep-sea sector as well, with offshore fishing now constituting the focus of the industry.

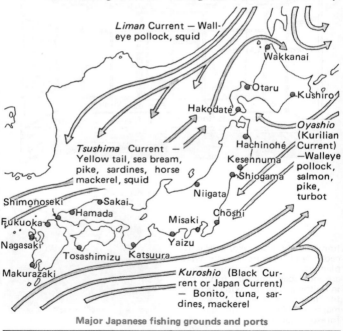

Major Japanese fishing grounds and ports

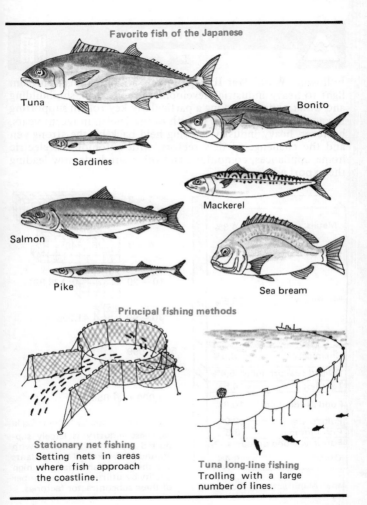

Favorite fish of the Japanese

Tuna

Sardines

Bonito

Mackerel

Salmon

Pike

Sea bream

Principal fishing methods

Stationary net fishing
Setting nets in areas where fish approach the coastline.

Tuna long-line fishing
Trolling with a large number of lines.

Following World War II, Japan made a major transition from light to heavy industrial development, with steel, shipbuilding and other exports playing a particularly key role in supporting the accelerated economic growth of the 1960s. In recent years, however, heavy industry is being held back by the strong yen and the challenge of new sectors, with automobiles, electric home appliances, computers, and other products now leading the export advance.

Japan Manufacturing Industries	
Metals:	14.3%
Machinery:	38.5%
Chemicals:	8.0%
Oil and coal products:	5.4%
Textiles:	4.5%
Food production:	10.8%
Pulp, paper:	2.9%
Fish farming:	3.5%
Forestry, wood products:	2.7%
Other:	9.4%

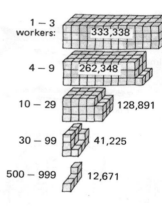

1 – 3 workers:	333,338
4 – 9	262,348
10 – 29	128,891
30 – 99	41,225
500 – 999	12,671
1,000 +	650

Number of Plants by Worker Scale

Japanese industry is largely supported by small factories with around 10 workers. The big plants cut their costs and maintain high quality by utilizing a large number of these subcontractor factories.

The four industrial zones on the Pacific Ocean side of Japan

The four industrial zones on the Pacific Ocean side of Japan (the *Keihin, Chūkyō, Hanshin* and *Kita-Kyūshū* zones) account for about one half of the shipment value of Japan's manufacturing industries. The area along the coastline which connects these zones is also known as the "Pacific Ocean Belt Zone."

Cities with over 100 billion yen in annual shipment value

1 Hitachi
2 Chiba
3 Ichihara
4 Tōkyō
5 Sagamihara
6 Kawasaki
7 Yokohama
8 Yokosuka
9 Fujisawa
10 Fuji
11 Hamamatsu
12 Toyota
13 Nagoya
14 Yokkaichi

15 Kyōto
16 Ōsaka
17 Higashi-Ōsaka
18 Sakai
19 Wakayama
20 Amagasaki
21 Kōbé
22 Himeji
23 Kurashiki
24 Fukuyama
25 Hiroshima
26 Kita-Kyūshū
27 Ōita

Four Major Industrial Zones	(as of 1993)
A Keihin (Tōkyō, Kanagawa):	14.6%
B Chūkyō (Aichi, Mié):	13.7%
C Hanshin (Ōsaka, Hyōgo):	12.0%
D Kita-Kyūshū (Fukuoka):	2.5%
Other Industrial Zones	(as of 1985)
E Keiyō (Chiba):	2.6%
F Tōkai (Shizuoka):	4.6%
G Setouchi (Okayama, Hiroshima, Ehimé):	6.3%
H Hokuriku (Niigata, Toyama, Fukui, Ishikawa):	3.8%
I Other:	37.4%

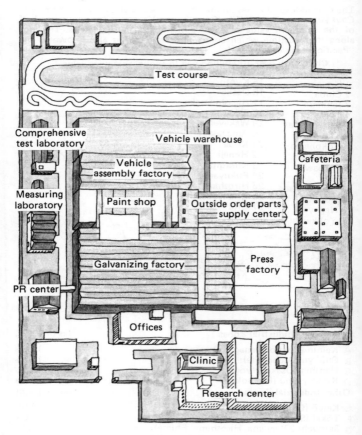

Test course

Comprehensive test laboratory

Vehicle warehouse

Cafeteria

Vehicle assembly factory

Measuring laboratory

Paint shop

Outside order parts supply center

Galvanizing factory

Press factory

PR center

Offices

Clinic

Research center

Automobile plants

A Day in the Life of a Plant Worker

Commuting to work

When plants are located in the suburbs, most workers commute by car. Special shuttle buses are often provided for those who must travel from a nearby station to the plant.

Meals

Meals are always eaten at the plant cafeteria. There are no distinctions in such cafeterias by position, with the plant manager and average line worker eating the same dishes.

Radio calisthenics

At most plants, workers perform light calisthenics along to music on the radio before their work day begins. Morning assemblies and meetings are also quite common.

Circle activities

Plants provide tennis courts, gymnasiums, and other sports facilities on their grounds, which are available for use after work hours. Larger plants help the workers organize sports teams and competition.

See vol.8 chapter 1 "A day of a Salaryman"

Japan's machine industry boasts one of the highest levels of mechanization and robotization in the world. Companies have used massive scale automation to cut costs, in the guest to heighten their price competitiveness.

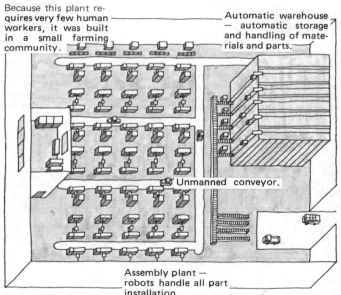

Because this plant requires very few human workers, it was built in a small farming community.

Automatic warehouse — automatic storage and handling of materials and parts.

Unmanned conveyor.

Assembly plant — robots handle all part installation.

Unmanned Plants

There are some plants where thorough automation has eliminated the need for human workers. Unmanned conveyors carry materials from the warehouses, while all work from machining thorough assembly is handled by robots — turning out superb quality products at low cost.

Painting robots

Japanese Word Processors

The Japanese language, which is comprised of a combination of three different alphabets *(kanji, hiragana* and *katakana),* was once considered a realm impossible for word processing. Today, however, many high-precision Japanese word processors are available at low prices, and are being combined with computer functions to make a major contribution to office automation.

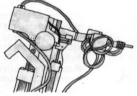

Spot welding robots

Industrial robots

The development of various types of computer-controlled industrial robots has made major reductions in product cost.

Janitor robots

These robots clean up the halls of buildings late at night.

Reception robots

Some robots are designed to serve coffee to customers.

JAPAN'S DISTRIBUTION SYSTEM

流通のしくみ

The distribution routes for agricultural and industrial goods on the way to the consumer are quite complex, and tend to force up prices, make it difficult for foreign companies to establish local footholds, and create other problems. As a result, simplification of the distribution system looms as a pressing theme for the Japanese economy.

Rice

Farm

Japan agricultural cooperatives

Government

Rice retailer

Consumer

High-quality rice is not channeled through the government, and usually wholesaled directly to the rice shops by individual farms or the cooperatives.

Japan agricultural cooperatives are part of a huge organization which almost all farms belong to. Besides produce distribution, these associations are also active in banking, insurance, and other sectors.

Rice is the main staple food of the Japanese people. The government buys up all rice, for sale at prices lower than at what it is purchased. This has resulted in economic stability for farming households, although the cost of this arrangement has generated a heavy financial burden for the nation.

Vegetables

Farm

Vegetable market

Vegetable shop

Agricultural cooperative

Fish

Consumer

Port

Wholesale market

Fisherman's cooperative association

Fish shop

Vegetables and fish are carried primarily by truck from the producing centers to Tōkyō, Ōsaka, and other big cities. With the price of fish especially swayed by freshness, trucks often speed down expressways late at night to make it to the market by dawn.

Tōkyō Central Wholesale Market

Central wholesale markets are large-scale fresh produce markets established in cities with populations of over 200,000, while all prices are determined by bidding *(seri)*. The Tōkyō Central Wholesale Market in *Tsukiji* is the largest scale market in Japan, handing about 2300 tons of marine products in a day.

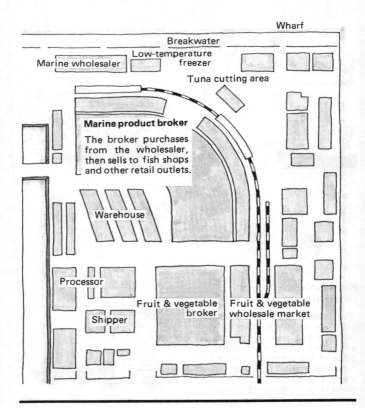

A Day at the Wholesale Market

Delivery
(from the previous afternoon through late at night)
The produce is carried in by ship, truck and train, and lined up at the wholesale area before the bidding begins.

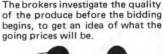

The brokers investigate the quality of the produce before the bidding begins, to get an idea of what the going prices will be.

Bidding (5 — 6:00 a.m.)
In the presence of the wholesalers, bidding is held between brokers and participating purchasers (large-scale consumers or processors who purchase directly from the wholesaler) to determine the price.

Broker Market (6:00 a.m. to noon)
The brokers carry the produce they have purchased to shops inside the market, and sell to retailers.

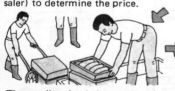

The retailers haul the produce by truck or other means to their own stores. There are many *sushi* shops and restaurants which purchase directly from the market.

Just outside the market are rows of shops offering many different fresh or processed products. These shops are more oriented toward individual customers.

INDUSTRIAL PRODUCTS DISTRIBUTION ROUTE

The distribution route for industrial products in Japan is distinguished by: 1) The large amount of corporate export operations handled by trading companies; and 2) the frequent instances of complex tangles of wholesalers.

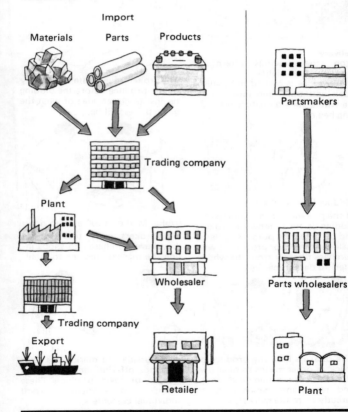

Different Retailers

Akihabara Electric Appliance District

The *Akihabara* district of Tōkyō is famous for its rows and rows of electric appliance stores, which sell products at far below market prices. Available here are refrigerators, televisions, audio and video equipment, the latest in computers, and virtually any other electric product as well.

Ueno Ameyoko

A distinctive shopping district in the *Ueno* district of Tōkyō which got its start immediately after World War II as a black market for U.S. army surplus goods.
Today, a vast range of products, from processed foods to clothing, can be obtained here at bargain basement prices.

Shinjuku Camera Shops

A large number of camera discount shops have sprung up around *Shinjuku* Station in Tōkyō. In addition to cameras and video cameras, they also offer calculators, watches, video game software, and other products.

24-Hour Supermarkets

In the big cities, more and more people are active late at night. This trend has led to a sharp increase in the number of 24-hour convenience stores.

TRADE

貿易

Blessed with few natural resources, Japan has used the rapid industrialization in the postwar era to expand its economic might as a trading nation — importing materials, and exporting finished products. However, with its trade surplus reaching an unprecedented scale on the strength of sinking oil prices and the strong yen, Japan is now moving to voluntarily control its exports, increase imports, and make other efforts to achieve a balance of trade payments.

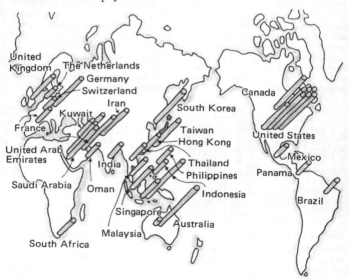

Japan's Major Trading Partners
(Unit: one pole = 100 million dollars)

Types of Exports

Machinery and equipment 74%
(Automobiles/office equipment/
boats/VTR/prime movers/radios/
televisions/metal machining equip-
ment/motorcycles)

Metals and metal products 8%
(Metals and metal products)

Other 6%
(Rubber tire tubes/toys)

Textiles and textile products 2%
(Synthetic textiles/clothing/
cotton goods/synthetic thread)

Chemical products 7%
(Elements & chemical compounds/
Man-made plastics)

Foods 0.5%
(Marine produce)

Non-ferrous metal products 1%
(Ceramics)

Types of Imports

(as of 1997)

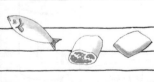

Mineral fuels 18%
(Oil/petroleum products/coal)

Other 22%
(Non-ferrous metals/textile pro-
ducts/non-monetary gold/steel)

Foods 13%
(Marine products/meats/corn/
wheat)

Machinery and equipment 28%
(Transport equipment/office
equipment/precision instruments)

Other materials 5%
(Lumber/soybeans)

Chemical products 18%
(Medical products)

Metal materials 2%
(Iron ore/non-ferrous metals)

Textile materials 0.4%
(Cotton/wool)

POLLUTION

公害

The rapid industrialization of the 1960s resulted in various pollution problems around Japan. Today, how to protect and cultivate the environment, which has been damaged for the sake of economic development, is a crucial theme for the nation.

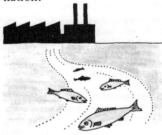

Minamata Disease

Mercury-laced plant drainage water was dumped into the sea, with the local people who consumed fish from that area gradually struck down by severe mercury poisoning. Even today, over 10,000 people continue to battle this disease.

"Itai-Itai" Disease

A pollution disease caused by cadmium in mine drainage water. With the disease causing agonizing bone pain, patients would cry out *"itai itai"* ("it hurts, it hurts!"), leading to the name.

Arsenic Milk Poisoning

An incident in which arsenic was inadvertently mixed into the powdered milk of a leading milk company. A large number of infants who were given this milk developed serious poisoning symptoms.

Major Environmental Pollution Diseases

Urban Pollution

The residents of large Japanese cities must put up with the following types of pollution:

Noise

Vibration

Air pollution

Water pollution

Soil pollution

Ground settling

日本の伝統産業

During the *Edo* period, a wide range of traditional technical arts were promoted in order to swell the revenues of the feudal clans. Many of these techniques have been carried on to the current day, with master craftsmen turning out elaborate and highly distinctive products.

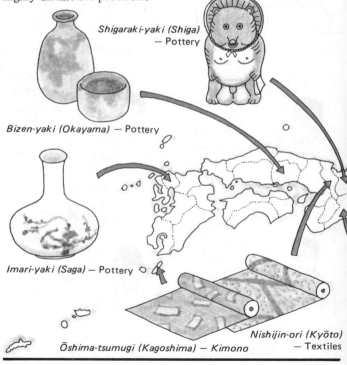

Shigaraki-yaki (Shiga) — Pottery

Bizen-yaki (Okayama) — Pottery

Imari-yaki (Saga) — Pottery

Ōshima-tsumugi (Kagoshima) — Kimono

Nishijin-ori (Kyōto) — Textiles

Echizen-washi (Fukui) — Japanese paper

Wajima-nuri (Ishikawa) — Lacquerware

Nambu Tekki (Iwaté) — Ironware

Miyagi Kokeshi (Miyagi) — Wooden dolls

Mashiko-yaki (Tochigi) — Pottery

Iga-kumihimo (Mié) — Braided cord

Kamakura-bori (Kanagawa) — Wood carvings

Making Pottery	Making Tsumugi (Fine Kimono Fabric)

Clay kneaded with water is placed on a potter's wheel, and shaped with the hands as it is turned.

Silk thread is created one strand at a time.

The piece is placed in a kiln for baking.

The finished thread is placed in a kettle with *ai* (indigo plant) dye.

The finished pottery is brush painted.

The dyed thread is woven on a hand loom.

Pottery: vol.1 p.38, vol.5 p.54, vol.6 p.162 **Tsumugi:** vol.6 p.168

Making Puppets	Making Japanese Paper

One craftsman makes the face.

Mulberry tree bark is boiled to create the ingredients.

Another applies the hair.

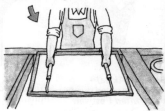

A bamboo frame to take out one sheet of paper at a time. This is known as *kamisuki* (papermaking).

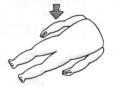

Another fasions the body.

A fitter puts the entire puppet together, and dresses it in proper costume.

The painted paper is pressed and dried.

REGIONAL FOLK TOYS

郷土玩具

The Japanese are fond of traditional toys, with those based on regional festivals or legends often highly prized as local souvenirs.

Bonten (Akita) — miniatures used during the *Bonten* Festival.

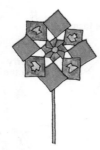

Fūsha (Aichi) — windmills.

Santai-Mikoshi (Hiroshima) — miniatures of the palanquin shrines used in festival.

Pūyaré (Ehimé) — ox devil appearing in the *Warei* Festival.

Iwai Tai (Shizuoka) — the seabream is considered a fish of good fortune.

Momotarō Shinzō (Fukui) — image of the hero of a famous fairytale.

POLITICS
AND
ECONOMICS

·

政治・経済

OVERVIEW

While Japan adopts the same type of parliamentarian government as Great Britain, the history of this political system is only five decades old, having been created after the end of World War II.

With the *Meiji* restoration of 1867, Japan underwent a transformation from a feudal country dominated by the *Tokugawa* shogunate into a modernizing nation. The German empire was used as reference in this effort, with Japan also adopting a political system of centralized authority, with the emperor at the pinnacle. Supported by this solid system, Japan rose to become the most powerful imperialist nation in Asia, and eventually invaded China, Korea, and other neighboring nations.

After its defeat in World War II, Japan's political system underwent sweeping changes under the U.S.-directed move to democratic rule. This new parliamentary system began to take root from the 1950s, and sparked the start of Japan's incredible economic growth.

The current Japanese political system is characterized by the following areas:

(1) Symbolic Emperor

Before World War II the Emperor was regarded as the embodiment of all power, and believed to be a "living god." After Japan's defeat, the Emperor personally announced that he was a human being, and relinquished all real power. Today, the Emperor is active in international exchange and other diplomatic activities, and serves as the figurehead of the Japanese nation.

(2) Renouncement of War

Japan is the only nation to ever suffer an atomic attack, and its constitution states that the country shall maintain no means of external invasion, and renounce war. As a result, the role of the Japanese armed forces (the Self-Defense Forces) is limited strictly to defense.

(3) Government

Except for a very short period soon after the end of the war, until 1993 Japan's postwar politics were basically dominated by similar political philosophies. Two major groupings, the Liberal Party and the Democratic Party, united in 1955 to form the Liberal Democratic Party, which remained in power until 1993. The LDP's fall from grace came after defections which gave rise to new parties, and the loss of its majority in a general election. Yet in the following years a chastened LDP has made a partial comeback. In 1995 the LDP formed a coalition government with the two other parties, the Japan Socialist Party (which had been the most important opposition party for many years) and the New party Sakigaké. In 1999 the LDP formed a new coalition with the Liberal Party and Komeito.

(4) Bureaucratic Mechanism

Japan has developed an extremely strong bureaucratic mechanism, with bureaucrats playing a pivotal role in energizing the economy, and determining the political flow.

THE CONSTITUTION

憲法

Japan's first modern constitution was the "Japan Imperial Constitution," enacted by the Emperor Meiji in 1889. The present constitution was promulgated in 1946, and is a democratic document based on the three pillars of 1) the sovereignty of the people; 2) respect of fundamental human rights; and 3) pacifism.

The people (holding sovereignty)

Elections

Supreme Court review

Public opinion

Enactment of law

The Diet

Impeachment of judges

Dissolving the Lower House

Designation of the Prime Minister
Cabinet confidence resolution

Judicial review

Judicial appointment

The courts

Administrative measure hearing

The Cabinet

Japan's Political System

Separation of the three powers (administration, legislation and judicature), parliamentarian, and other aspects of the Japanese political system are outlined in the constitution.

Differences Between Japan Imperial Constitution and the current Constitution

Sovereignty of the people

Sovereignty has been transferred from the Emperor to the people, with political decisions conducted by a Diet of elected politicians and a cabinet approved by the Diet. Today, the Emperor is the symbol of the entire Japanese nation.

Fundamental human rights

Freedom, suffrage, social rights, fair legal treatment, and other fundamental human rights are guaranteed under the current constitution. Before World War II, individuals or groups who opposed the Imperial system were fiercely repressed, while the right to vote was also restricted.

Pacifism

Under Article 9 of the Constitution, Japan renounces both war and military forces. As a result, there is a constant debate over whether or not the current Self-Defense Forces (equipped at the largest scale of any military force in Asia) are in violation of the Constitution.

Obligations of the People

The fundamental obligations of the Japanese people include giving their children an education, working, and paying taxes. Japan, a nation which officially rejects the need for military forces, has no compulsory military service system, with the Self-Defense Forces comprised entirely of volunteers.

DIET

国会

Japan's National Diet is comprised of the House of Representatives and the House of Councillors. The major role of the House of Councillors is to reexamine decisions handed down by the House of Representatives. The House of Representatives has 500 members, each serving four-year terms. The Prime Minister, however, has the right to dissolve the House at any time. The House of Councillors has 252 members, each serving six-year terms with no dissolution.

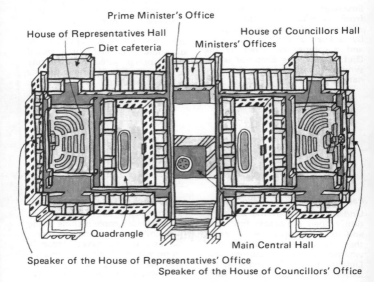

Prime Minister's Office

House of Representatives Hall

Diet cafeteria

Ministers' Offices

House of Councillors Hall

Quadrangle

Main Central Hall

Speaker of the House of Representatives' Office

Speaker of the House of Councillors' Office

Layout of the Diet Building

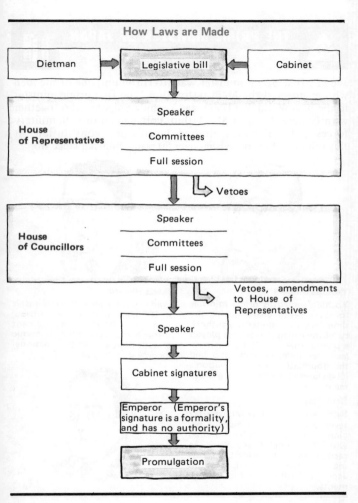

How Laws are Made

Dietman → Legislative bill ← Cabinet

House of Representatives
- Speaker
- Committees
- Full session

→ Vetoes

House of Councillors
- Speaker
- Committees
- Full session

→ Vetoes, amendments to House of Representatives

Speaker

Cabinet signatures

Emperor (Emperor's signature is a formality, and has no authority)

Promulgation

THE PRIME MINISTER OF JAPAN

日本の総理大臣

Japan's first prime minister was Itō Hirobumi, one of the men who engineered the Meiji restoration. The first prime minister in the post World War II era was Yoshida Shigeru, who together with General Douglas MacArthur, commander of U.S. military forces in the Far East, drafted Japan's new constitution. At this printing, there have been over 50 prime minister since Itō.

Yoshida Shigeru

Yoshida served as prime minister for over seven years, during the time Japan was under the authority of the Allied Powers. He played a pivotal role in helping Japan regain her independence, and laid the foundation for the nation's long-standing conservative government.

Ikeda Hayato

Ikeda first became Prime Minister in 1960, and made a key contribution to Japan's development through his accelerated economic growth policies and the "national income-doubling plan."

Satō Eisaku

Satō served as Prime Minister for seven years and eight months, beginning in 1964. He was honored with the Nobel Peace Prize, in recognition of his efforts in securing the return of Okinawa to Japan and other notable achievements.

Tanaka Kakuei

Tanaka assumed the post in 1972, and made major political contributions through his visit to the People's Republic of China and other activities. In 1974, however, he was forced from office by accusations of monetary kickbacks, leading to his official arrest in 1976 surrounding the purchase of military aircraft.

Nakasoné Yasuhiro

Nakasoné became Japan's prime minister in 1982. He showed his greatest strengths in the field of diplomacy, such as the hosting of the 1986 Tōkyō Summit.

Fukuda Takeo

Fukuda became prime minister in 1976. He is noted for signing the Sino-Japanese peace and friendship treaty, and was a major force in helping the Japanese economy recover from the first oil crisis.

Ōhira Masayoshi

Ōhira became prime minister in 1978. He embarked as a champion of fiscal reform, but died of heart failure during election campaigning in 1980.

Hosokawa Morihiro

Hosokawa worked as a newspaper reporter, then became a prefectural governor. He helped found the Japan New Party in 1992. During elections the following year, the Liberal Democratic Party was defeated after 38 years in power without a break. Hosokawa was named Prime Minister and headed a coalition government that did not include the Liberal Democrats.

The Cabinet is an administrative body comprised of the Prime Minister and other ministers of state. The Prime Minister is elected from the political party in power at the time. The Cabinet is a pivotal body which commands the vast organization of government offices, and keeps Japan on the move.

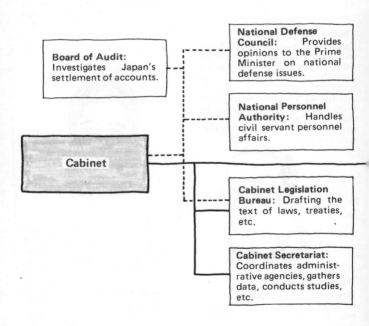

Board of Audit: Investigates Japan's settlement of accounts.

National Defense Council: Provides opinions to the Prime Minister on national defense issues.

National Personnel Authority: Handles civil servant personnel affairs.

Cabinet

Cabinet Legislation Bureau: Drafting the text of laws, treaties, etc.

Cabinet Secretariat: Coordinates administrative agencies, gathers data, conducts studies, etc.

Prime Minister's Office: Coordinates the work of all administrative agencies.

Ministry of Justice: In charge of legal affairs.

Ministry of Foreign Affairs: Diplomacy and international politics.

Ministry of Finance: In charge of financial affairs.

Ministry of Education, Culture and Science: Works to further Japanese education, culture and science.

Ministry of Health and Welfare: In charge of national health and medical affairs.

Ministry of Agriculture, Forestry and Fisheries: Coordinates the farming, forestry and fishing industries.

Ministry of Construction: Oversees civil engineering projects, national land planning, and other construction-related sectors.

Ministry of Transport: Passenger and cargo transport.

Ministry of Posts and Telecommunications: In charge of the postal system and general communications.

Ministry of Labor: Coordinates labor-management relations, and the general range of labor problems.

Ministry of International Trade and Industry: In charge of problems of trade and industry.

Ministry of Home Affairs: Offers leadership for local municipalities.

Map of Kasumigaseki government office district in Tōkyō

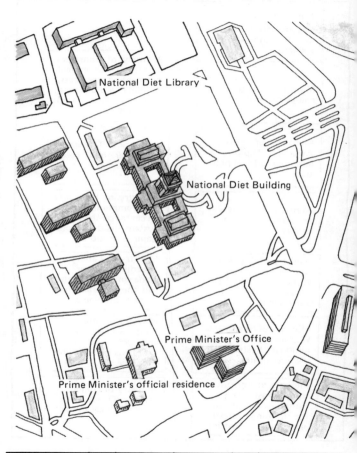

National Diet Library

National Diet Building

Prime Minister's Office

Prime Minister's official residence

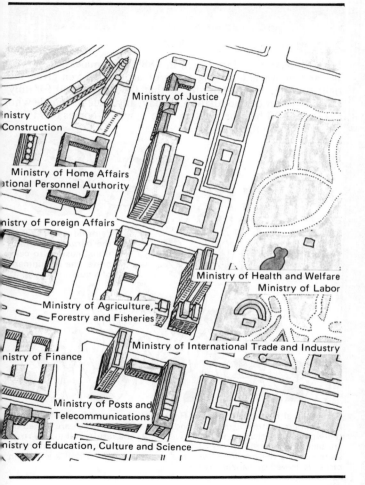

Ministry of Justice

nistry
Construction

Ministry of Home Affairs
ational Personnel Authority

nistry of Foreign Affairs

Ministry of Health and Welfare
Ministry of Labor

Ministry of Agriculture,
Forestry and Fisheries

Ministry of International Trade and Industry

nistry of Finance

Ministry of Posts and
Telecommunications

nistry of Education, Culture and Science

173

Japan's election system began in 1889, with males 25 years of age and above and paying taxes of at least 15 yen given the right to vote. The electorate at that time accounted for only 1.1% of the entire population. Today, any male or female who has turned 20 has the right to vote — which comes to 71% of the overall population.

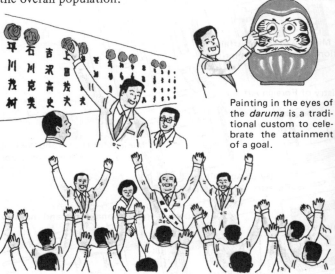

Painting in the eyes of the *daruma* is a traditional custom to celebrate the attainment of a goal.

For national elections (House of Representatives and House of Councillors), papers written names of candidates with the brush are pasted on the walls of political party headquarters. As the results roll in, red roses are placed above the names of the winners. When the number of party seats exceeds the previous level, the eyes of a *daruma* doll are filled in black, followed by *banzai* cheers.

The House of Representatives consists of 300 electoral districts nation-wide and 11 blocks — a total of 500 seats. The House of Councillors is a combination of nationwide based on proportional representation, and regional districts and contains a total of 252 seats. Each member serves a six-year term, with half (126) elected every three years.

Victory in Japanese elections requires the three *"ban"*: *Jiban* ("foundation" — i.e., a support network), *kanban* ("sign" — i.e., recognition), and *kaban* ("satchel" — i.e., money).

In country towns where there are few events of interest, elections often come to resemble festivals. Members of supporter's organizations take off from work to campaign for their favorite candidate, running around town until late at night to help drum up support.

There are increasing instances of sons running for the seats of their retiring Dietmen fathers, in order to carry on the network of support groups developed over the years. The majority of Japanese politicians consist of these "second generation" members, as well as bureaucratic leaders who choose to run for office.

New candidates go to great lengths to boost their recognition, such as attending the weddings and funerals of local residents. In contrast, there are some Diet members who have developed such solid grass root support that they hardly need to hit the campaign trail at all.

JAPAN'S POLITICAL PARTIES

政党

Political parties are simply political groups made up of various people with common principles, opinions, or political motives. In addition to the Liberal Democratic Party, which was launched in 1955, the Social Democratic Party, launched in 1945 as the Japan Socialist Party,and the Shinshintō (New Frontier) launched in 1994, there are also several relatively new parties, called mini-parties, with much smaller numbers of members . Each of the various parties, carries out intense election campaigns with the goal of sending as many of its candidates to the National Diet (parliament) as possible. Finally, as a result of these national elections, the party whose members constitute the majority of seats in the Diet wins the right to operate the national government. However, if no single party is able to acquire a majority of seats, then a coalition government is formed, and the cabinet is made up of members of multiple parties.

Political Independents

This designation refers to voters who, in public opinion surveys etc., respond that they "do not support any particular political party". All such voters are not considered as simply having no interest in political matters, however, because this also includes persons who are disenchanted with all of the existing parties. In terms of their voting behavior, we find that in the 1995 unified local elections, independent candidates were elected as governors in both Tōkyō and Ōsaka.

Patrimonial Diet Members (or Second-generation Diet Members)

This refers to a politician whose father, mother, or other relative was a politician, and who has become a Diet member by succeeding to the forerunner's strong political base. Patrimonial Diet members comprised 25% of all members elected in the 1993 general election, and the percentage was 41% for members of the LDP. While patrimonial candidates tend to stand a greater chance of being elected than do first-time candidates in general, conversely this can be said to narrow the path available for promising new candidates.

The History of Party Government in Japan

The principal framework for Japan's post-war government was established in 1955. Under this system, the government was operated by two parties, the LDP and the Socialist Party (precursor to the Social Democratic Party of Japan). However, because the Socialist Party was unable to win more than about half as many seats as the LDP, in reality the Japanese government was long controlled by the LDP alone. Then, during the 1993 election campaign the LDP split up, and in 1994 a coalition government was formed by the LDP, SDP, and Sakigaké. This brought to a close of the so-called "1955 structure" which had continued for the previous 38 years. Further, in 1994 the members of various minority parties banded together to form the Shinshintō (New Frontier Party), which dealt a massive blow to the LDP by winning more seats than the LDP in the 1995 Upper House election. In 1998, the New Frontier Party (Shinshintō) dissolved, and in 1999 a conservative alliance was formed between the Liberal Party (Jiyūtō) and Liberal Democratic Party (Jimintō), and Komeito. On the other hand, a new liberal party called the Democratic Party of Japan (Minshutō) was formed, becoming the main opposition party. The political party system in Japan is currently in a period of transition, and it is likely that more time will be required before a new political structure is established.

● **Party Activities**

The objective of political parties is to capture a majority of seats in elections and thereby control the administration of the government.

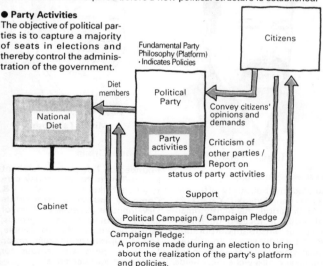

Fundamental Party Philosophy (Platform)
· Indicates Policies

Political Party

Party activities

Diet members

National Diet

Cabinet

Citizens

Convey citizens' opinions and demands

Criticism of other parties / Report on status of party activities

Support

Political Campaign / Campaign Pledge

Campaign Pledge:
    A promise made during an election to bring about the realization of the party's platform and policies.

The Japanese business world is characterized by six major corporate groups — *Mitsubishi, Mitsui, Sumitomo, Fuyō, Sanwa* and *Ichikan*. The combined sales of these groups total 150 trillion yen, or about 16% of the sales of all Japanese companies, and they play a leading role in the nation's economic activity.

Iwasaki Yatarō

Mitsui Takatoshi

The Mitsubishi Group

Founded by politically affiliated businessman Iwasaki Yatarō in the Meiji period, this tightly organized group is focused on Mitsubishi Bank, Mitsubishi Corporation and Mitsubishi Heavy Industries. It boasts particular strength in the banking and heavy chemical fields.

The Mitsui Group

Founded by Edo period merchant Mitsui Takatoshi, and today centered in Sakura Bank, Mitsui & Company and Mitsui Real Estate Development Company. Two of Japan's leading corporate groups, Mitsui is known for its people, and Mitsubishi for its organization. In short, both are famous for their top-flight personnel.

Sumitomo Masatomo

The Sumitomo Group

Founded by Sumitomo Masatomo, a prominent merchant of the Edo period. Together with the Mitsui family, the history of Sumitomo exceeds even that of Rothchild's. Focal companies are Sumitomo Bank, Sumitomo Metal Industries and Sumitomo Chemical Company. The group is distinguished by its massive financial power and highly unified structure.

Yasuda Zenjirō

The Fuyō Group

A group descended from the Yasuda financial combine of the prewar era, founded by Yasuda Zenjirō, a banking giant of the Meiji and Taisho eras. The central companies are Fuji Bank and the Marubeni Corporation. Many of the group's members are large independent companies, making its unity comparatively weak.

Kounoiké Zen'emon

The Sanwa Group

Rooted in the Kounoikeya family (founded by Kounoiké Zen'emon in 1619), this group is even older than the Mitsui family. The pivotal firm is Sanwa Bank, and its ranks also include Hitachi Zōsen (Shipbuilding), Ubé Industries, Teijin Ltd., and other major companies.

Shibusawa Eiichi

The Ichikan Group

Founded by Shibusawa Eiichi, the first-generation president of Japan's first bank — the Dai-Ichi Kokuritsu Bank (founded in 1873). The central companies are the Dai-Ichi Kangyō Bank (created through a merger of the Dai-Ichi Bank and Kangyō Bank in 1971) and C. Itoh & Company. Membership includes 46 companies, making this Japan's largest corporate group.

The Japanese economy, which hit rock bottom with the defeat in World War II, began to truly regain its feet on the strength of special procurements during the Korean War. It then set forth on a burst of double-digit annual economic growth which was sustained until the first oil crisis in 1973. This accelerated rise in economic strength has also created various problems in many different sectors.

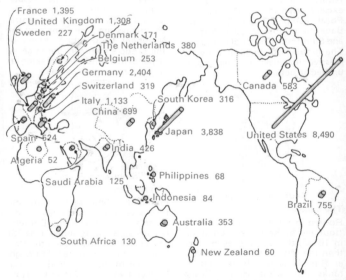

France 1,395
United Kingdom 1,308
Sweden 227
Denmark 171
The Netherlands 380
Belgium 253
Germany 2,404
Switzerland 319
Canada 583
Italy 1,133
South Korea 316
China 699
Spain 624
Japan 3,838
United States 8,490
Algeria 52
India 426
Saudi Arabia 125
Philippines 68
Indonesia 84
Brazil 755
South Africa 130
Australia 353
New Zealand 60

Unit / A billion dollar   1998

World GNP Map

Shift from Agriculture to Service

In 1955, about 40% of all employed Japanese were engaged in agriculture, forestry or fisheries related work. This has dropped to under 10 % today, with nearly 60 % of the labor force now employed in service industries.

Urban Population Concentration

The exodus of young people to the cities accompanying Japan's rapid industrialization has created severe difficulties in maintaining effective farm management. Other problems resulting from this trend include environmental destruction, skyrocketing land prices, and more.

Rising Commodity Prices

The increase rate in prices caused by the inflation of the accelerated growth period constantly outstripped the wage increase rate. As a result, while Japan has expanded her GNP and joined the ranks of economic superpowers, a contradiction exists in that the lifestyle of the average Japanese has not become affluent to a comparable degree.

Sharp Increase in Durable Consumer Goods

The ownership rate of electric refrigerators and color television more or less reached 100% in 1975, while passenger car ownership went over the 50% line in 1980. In short, the Japanese are literally awash in consumer goods in their daily lifestyles.

THE ECONOMIC LIFESTYLE OF THE JAPANESE

日本人の経済生活

Compared to other nations, Japan is a country with limited gaps in personal wealth. The majority of the Japanese consider themselves "middle class," and strive to lead a lifestyle appropriate for this level.

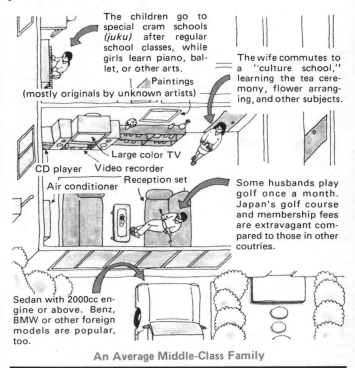

The children go to special cram schools *(juku)* after regular school classes, while girls learn piano, ballet, or other arts.

Paintings (mostly originals by unknown artists)

The wife commutes to a "culture school," learning the tea ceremony, flower arranging, and other subjects.

Large color TV

CD player   Video recorder

Air conditioner   Reception set

Some husbands play golf once a month. Japan's golf course and membership fees are extravagant compared to those in other coutries.

Sedan with 2000cc engine or above. Benz, BMW or other foreign models are popular, too.

An Average Middle-Class Family

Zai-Tech (Financial Engineering)

The average Japanese family has about 8.4 million yen in savings, a very high figure compared to the rest of the world. The art of *zai-tech* (using these savings to generate profits through stock, real estate and other investment) is experiencing a major boom in Japan today.

One of the most popular art of Zai-Tech is stock. But, in the years since the collapse of the bubble economy, the prices of many stocks have fallen sharply, and several people have suffered large losses. Real estate prices have also dropped by a large margin.

Soaring land prices, meanwhile, have made it impossible for a normal businessman to purchase a home in Tōkyō. People take the money they would otherwise use for a house to buy fancy cars, go on luxurious overseas trips, and other pleasures.

Back when the Japanese economy was in good shape, a trend for people to leave Japan to spend their retirement overseas began. At present, however, with the extremely low interest rates for savings and uncertainty about the future of retirement pensions, it is difficult to even consider doing such a thing.

With the rise in the value of the yen since the fall of 1985, the Japanese economy has arrived at a major historical crossroads. But, the result was the creation of the so-called "Bubble Economy" which eventually collapsed in 1991, severely damaging the Japanese economy. The value of the yen also dropped. However, the current account surplus continued to grow, and there was considerable pressure from the US and European countries to deal with this imbalance.

Building Overseas Plants
In industries which have seen restrictions slapped on their exports because of trade friction with Japan, local production is rapidly becoming a vital theme. With automakers at the fore, Japanese-style plants have begun to pop up all around the United States.

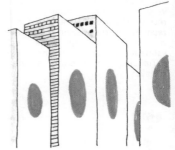

Positive Overseas Investment
Reflecting the strength of the yen, Japanese companies are buying up premiere real estate in many major U.S. cities. It is even being said that, in time, the majority of the famous New York skyline may fall into Japanese hands.

Globalization of the Japanese Economy

Japanese companies can no longer be assured of sustaining stable growth by concentrating on the manufacture of products at home for export abroad.

What has the Strong Yen Changed?

Depressed Heavy Industry

Steel, shipbuilding and other heavy industries have been hard hit by the price competition with the newly industrializing countries, and suffered worsened business conditions as a result.

1) Collapse of the Bubble
2) From the end of the 1980's to the beginning of the 1990's
3) This was the "Bubble Economy" and the damage caused by its collapse has resulted in a financial system on the verge of a severe crisis.

Japayuki-san

The strong yen attracted people from Southeast Asia and other developing regions, who travel to Japan to work without official permits. The women often work in bars or red-light districts, while the men work at waiters, construction workers, and other menial labor. These people have been nicknamed *Japayuki-san* (those who go to Japan), a play on the term *Karayuki-san* — a reference to Japanese women who (in years long past) traveled to Southeast Asian nations to earn money as prostitutes.

I·N·D·E·X

For Your TraveLife

英文 **日本絵とき事典10**

ILLUSTRATED
TODAY'S JAPAN

初版発行	1988年 1月 1日
改訂9版	2000年 9月 1日
	(Sep. 1, 2000 9th edition)
編 集 人	黒澤明夫
発 行 人	青木玲二
発 行 所	JTB
印 刷 所	JTB印刷

企 画	JTB出版事業局 編集六部
編 集	るるぶ社 海外ガイドブック編集部
取材・編集協力	アーバン・トランスレーション
イラスト	松下正己
表紙デザイン	東 芳純
翻 訳	Dick Belcher

●JTB発行の図書のご注文は
JTB 出版販売センター ☎03-3477-9590
〒150-0043 東京都渋谷区道玄坂1-10-8 渋谷野村ビル7階
●本書の内容のお問合せは
るるぶ社 海外ガイドブック編集部 ☎03-5489-6172
〒150-0043 東京都渋谷区道玄坂1-10-8 渋谷野村ビル9階
●広告のお問合せは
JTB 出版事業局 広告部 ☎03-3477-9531
●ひらけば旅がはじまる JTB の出版案内
http://rurubu.com

禁無断転載・複製 © JTB 1997 Printed in Japan

004210 712123

ISBN4-533-00893-3